Performing the Roma Witch: Stereotype, Mythology, and Profit

GEORGE GOGA

Performing the Roma Witch: Stereotype, Mythology, and Profit

GEORGE GOGA

Dapper Sloth Press

Published by
Dapper Sloth Press | Buffalo, NY
geogoga.com
© 2019 George Goga

Cover design: Alfred Quitevis

Printed in the United States of America.

p-ISBN: 978-1-0925134-6-3

CONTENTS

For Richard Wesp, with gratitude.

Every life is many days, day after day. We walk
through ourselves, meeting robbers, ghosts, giants,
old men, young men, wives, widows, brothers-in-love,
but always meeting ourselves.

—James Joyce, *Ulysses*

Thou hast seen nothing yet.

—Miguel de Cervantes, *Don Quixote*

Preface

Well into the writing of this book, my mom turned to me and told me in a confiding tone that my connection to witchcraft was even closer than I could imagine. The research I was doing was great (mom has always been my number one fan), but there was something she had never told me before that I should now know. Tonight. She had once known a witch.

Her name was Da Gheorghita[1] and she lived in Urzicu-ta-Ionele, a small town in the south-western region of Roma-nia. She practiced witchcraft between 1940 and 1970 and came to be known as the village witch. At the time, the population of Urzicuta-Ionele was approximately 3,000, and my mom, who visited family every summer, would have been ten-years-old when she first encountered Gheorghita. She describes her as a kind, restrained woman who always had people over at her house. Although she didn't realize it at the time, this was because Gheorghita held consultations in her home, helping women work through a host of issues from fertility to infideli-ty. Mom describes seeing many people visiting Gheorghita, al-

---

1   In Romanian, "Da" is an affectionate term for "aunt."

ways coming with bags of food and drink, fresh eggs and meat. Many shouted greetings as they walked by her house on their way to work, asking the children who gathered in the street if she was home, and if not, when she would be. In town, everyone knew that Gheorghita woke up every morning at 3a.m. to prepare bread for her family, interspersing her client consultations with the realization that she had become responsible for feeding many of the townspeople with her kindness.

But this was only one of her responsibilities. Being the village witch carried a host of others, including the black and white magic she practiced, casting love spells and curses for her clients. She remedied *deochiul* (evil eye) in children, gave women advice from her storied career, and even told people's fortunes, reading their futures in the bottom of upside-down coffee cups. She never charged money, instead exchanging her knowledge of the occult for food, drink, and company. As mom played in the street with her friends, she cast her eyes toward Gheorghita's house, a plain, one-story structure still common in the Eastern European countryside, never quite sure what happened on the inside. Gheorghita was caring, and clearly loved the town's children. But what did she *do*?

In many ways, the history of witchcraft can be encapsulated in this question alone—in our human intrigue for knowing something beyond the obvious about the women labelled witches. In children this is pure, innocent curiosity, and the fact that mom and her friends repeatedly asked that question indicates the extent to which they were comfortable asking about the village witch's business. But in asking the same question, the history of witchcraft hasn't always been as kind, pursuing women for the greater public's inability to understand, empathize, or learn. This infrequently involved a calm conversation. On the contrary, it typically included male violence as a vague, incorrect answer to the same question history has always asked about the women it didn't first seek to understand. In many ways, the answer to *What did she do?* spurred on the great European Witch Craze, a histrionic, distinctly male reaction to the discomfort our early modern world had with women who resisted traditional definitions of domicile, gender roles, and the boredom of everyday life. Since then, the figure of the witch has adapted to our modern world, allowing women to repurpose the same identity we once sought to destroy through violence. Today, adopting the identity of the witch is an act of reclamation, of calling out, naming, and asserting a response to that distinctly male fear over women who cannot easily be classified.

But where did that innocent childhood curiosity go? And why has our world been unable to maintain this curiosity about women without turning to violence? Gheorghita was not only known as the village witch, but actively *claimed* this identity, priding herself on the fact that the love spells and curses, the binding and unbinding that helped her cure *deochiul* actually improved other people's lives. She made a difference; people knew and appreciated that. In Romania's deeply folkloric tradition, her role in the community was akin to the doctor's, the lawyer's—even the teacher's. Her access to the occult placed her in contact with everyone in Urzicuta-Ionele. This allowed her to transact business with the entire community, placing the emotional burden of hundreds of people onto her listening ears. By exchanging food and drink for knowledge of the occult, she also entered a bartering economy, marrying the realization that women didn't work with the fact that they were still responsible for putting food in their family's mouths.

Throughout women's history, this dependence has gone unstated, flying under the radar that is male need. The people of Urzicuta-Ionele were thankful for their dependence on Gheorghita and demonstrated their love by sharing her company, buying into her occult rituals, and compensating her with food and drink. They helped her feel needed. But this unstated dependence has also been burdensome since it isn't always the case that witches are believed, respected, or loved. Historically, they have been destroyed through physical and psychological violence, cast to the outskirts of society both physically and figuratively, a no-place where they could be silenced through social isolation. Often, they weren't even taken seriously. Today, the identity of the witch encourages women to name this unstated dependence and actively resist it. It helps women make others understand that their historical dependence on strong women hasn't always been compensated, respected, or even acknowledged. Perhaps for this reason has the identity become so empowering for so many in today's world. But it would be a mistake not to point out how young this acceptance is. Even Gheorghita, who lived some 80 years ago, would have interacted with people who dismissed her knowledge of the occult too hastily. Along with the figure of the witch, feminism has given this unstated dependence a name and a platform to speak out.

Writing this book has put me in touch with a side of my personal history that I hadn't seriously evaluated. Among many other things, graduate school has served as the stage for this exploration, allowing me to express these views in the context of a rich historical tradition of witchcraft in contemporary Romania, a country rooted in folklore and myth, in national symbols and strong women. Although celebratory in this book, the combination of these elements has also been used to disempower, and though the image we form of Gheorghita is one of acceptance and perseverance, it would be a mistake to let this anecdote cloud our considerations of witchcraft writ large, a dynamic that our world is allowing and slowly starting to accept, but is still sanctioning and speaking out against. I don't know what questions I'd ask Gheorghita if she were still alive today, though I suspect she'd be happy to share company and a traditional meal. I also don't know what she would think of our world's recent reclamation of witchcraft, inhabiting as we do a social media atmosphere where witches have even debuted on Facebook, Instagram, and Tumblr. What, for instance, would she say about the Roma witches profiled in this book? Although we have no way of knowing, I'd venture a guess that she'd probably be as accepting as ever, leaving us with the impression that the overwhelming social isolation our world forced women to experience on account of their witchcraft would not be reciprocated if they had been given a legitimate chance to respond.

I've asked my mom more details about Gheorghita, whom she vaguely remembers and whose memory has helped me sketch the portrait of a woman on whom many depended. Mom has always been one to strategically disclose details of family history. At this point in the story, she turned to me. She wanted me to know, before we moved any further, that in fact, Gheorghita had been her grandma. Growing up, mom had seen her only infrequently. She confided that, in the odd coincidences life throws our way, the names Gheorghita and George are more similar than dissimilar. I considered, nodding. Maybe that's the explanation after all.

Introduction

In much the same way that the American tourist first encounters the Roma through a mix of first-hand experience and cultural anecdotes, the American public experienced them—some seventy years earlier—through the writings of Joseph Mitchell. In his 1942 profile for *The New Yorker*, "King of Gypsies," Mitchell shares one of the first coherent images of Eastern European gypsies living in the United States. Mitchell's subject is Johnny Nikanov, the eponymous King of the Gypsies, whom he profiles in the whirlwind playground Nikanov calls home, New York City. Aside from the historicism Mitchell is known for, I quote the following passage at length for two reasons. The first is that it presents an anecdote about the gypsies largely sustained by myth and popular reporting. The second is that it uses this anecdote to make a value judgement about the gypsies that is then widely disseminated to the magazine's readership, primarily the American public. Aside from the impressive rhetorical lengths Mitchell goes to to characterize Johnny Nikanov, a man who's "been king of the gypsies off and on since he was a young man," Mitchell also admits that "A gypsy gets to be a king by calling himself one."

Describing how gypsies make money, Mitchell writes:

The women are the real breadwinners. All of them are *dukkerers*, or fortunetellers. They foretell the future by the interpretation of dreams and by the location of moles on the body, lines of the palm, and bumps on the head. This occupation is illegal in the city and they operate furtively...'If a sensible-acting woman goes to a gypsy, she gets her fortune told and that's the end of it. But when one of those thick babies comes along, the *dukkerer* gets down to work. Most of them use a swindle that's old as the hills. We call it the gypsy-switch or the wallet-switch and they call it the *hokkano baro*, the big trick. First of all the gypsy convinces the victim there's something wrong with her insides; usually they say it's cancer. This may take several visits; they like to work slow and get some fun out of it. Pretty soon the victim is so upset she'll do just about anything; when gypsies set their minds to it, they can be more scary than the stuff you'll see in the movies...Then the gypsy says that money's what's wrong, that the money the victim has been saving for years is unclean, un-holy, got the black mark on it. So the victim trots to the bank and withdraws her savings, every red cent, and gives it to the gypsy to be cleaned, or blessed. The gypsy rolls up the bills, sews them inside a little cloth bag, lights some dime-store candles, and blesses the bag with a lot of hocus-pocus. All the time the gypsy has another bag up her sleeve and this has a roll of blank paper in it. After a while she switches bags, and she sews the phony bag securely to the inside of the victim's dress over her heart, and she tells her to wear it that way seven days before opening it. At night she's supposed to put the dress with the bag on it under her pillow. That will make her well. And soon as the victim is out of sight the gypsy family packs up and moves. And a week later the victim runs howling to the police.'

From this anecdote alone, Mitchell establishes the ideological slant of his mythology. He presents the *dukkerer* as an object of dislike, enumerating the lengths she goes to defraud her client. In doing so, the *dukkerer* violates not only the law, but also the personal-ethical dilemma associated with scamming people out of their savings. This anecdote allows Mitchell to present the gypsy as fundamentally evil for transacting something she's clearly comfortable doing repeatedly to non-gypsies. But he doesn't stop there. In laying the groundwork for anti-gypsy sentiment in the United States, Mitchell's mythology suggests that:

1. Gypsy scam artists are typically female. In my reading, this is reserved for women because it's in touch with their traditionally emotive side.

2. The scam artists target other women. In my reading, this is because women are typically seen as more suggestible to scamming, which relies on a trust pact enacted between two women.

3. The scam artists locate their scam in the human body: "First of all the gypsy convinces the victim there's something wrong with her insides; usually they say it's cancer." In my reading, this suggests that the gypsy is not only in touch with the human core more than the non-gypsy (a subtle, yet powerful myth perpetuated about traditional, folksy gypsyism), but also because the gypsy is able to see beyond the physicality of the body and thus respond to different levels of meaning that the non-gypsy cannot understand about their own body.

4. The scam is founded on the transaction of money—typically cash, which is harder to trace and regulate than other forms of currency. In my reading, this suggests that the gypsy shares roles with the money changer

but does so under the acknowledgement that she is exchanging money for truth, for some knowledge beyond
the non-gypsy, which the non-gypsy can only experience by transacting cash for knowledge.

Overwhelmingly, Mitchell's anecdote presents the gypsy as a
scam artist, as someone who uses their deep attachment with
the core of human existence for evil. He also makes a series of
compelling (if deeply stereotypical) arguments about gypsyism
in the United States, but is careful to couch these arguments in
counterpoint to the institutions they violate. For instance, the
scam artist is first and foremost an "occupation [that] is illegal
in the city" and must "operate furtively." This places the ideological work of his stereotyping on institutions beyond himself
while also allowing him to play to these institutions for support.
It's difficult to estimate how far-reaching Mitchell's profile is,
but here it remains invaluable because it makes a value judgement about gypsies *living among us* that's then widely disseminated to the magazine's readership, the American public. In
doing so, it carries out ideological work as an interpreter of
gypsy life. Mitchell, a well-regarded journalist at the time of
publication, is seen as a cultural mediator between gypsies and
non-gypsies, thus lending him extreme credibility.

Mitchell is one of the first voices in American consciousness to represent the gypsies. He is thus seen as a cultural interlocutor, a lens through which the American public experiences
gypsy culture. But his profile of Johnny Nikanov is also deeply troubling for the historical anachronism it commits. In the
"Grammar of Hard Facts" published by the *Economist*, its writer
concludes that "Cockeye Johnny Nikanov, one of Mitchell's be-
loved profile subjects, was a composite character invented by
Mitchell" and goes on to demonstrate how "Mitchell regular-

ly altered experiences and quotations referred to in his stories. [He] did not think this light fictionalising would discredit his work." Although the *Economist* writer concedes that "it was not so unusual for *The New Yorker* to run composite profiles," they note that "the practice has long since been banned at the magazine." Of Mitchell, they conclude that, "[he] at least… felt his technique could conjure a major literary effect," citing the author himself, who claimed that [Nikanov] "'is truer to life than I would've been able to make him had he been a real person.'" Edginess really does sell.

This expose raises as many questions as it answers, about Mitchell and the relevance of his reporting as published in *The New Yorker*, but I'm most interested in the interplay between Mitchell's profile and the image of gypsy culture it creates, regardless of the historical, academic, and journalistic integrity it circumvents. Mitchell, who may have been quick to throw all of these out the window, nevertheless composes a prolific article on the Gypsy King whose effects continue to be felt in American consciousness today, a consciousness that takes a few moves from Mitchell's playbook when it comes to representing gypsy culture. It would be difficult to overstate the role that mythology played in this particular instance of anti-gypsyism, and to overstate the role it continues to play in today's representations of contemporary Roma culture.

Some seventy years later, Mitchell's reporting on gypsies would be eclipsed only by *Vice News*, the cultural interlocutor I'm concerned with in this book. *Vice News*, which serves to share "under-reported stories" with the world, interprets gypsy culture much in the same way that Mitchell interpreted it for an eager American readership in 1942. But I'm also interested in the institutions Mitchell presents the gypsies in violation to, and a great deal of the work I attempt to accomplish involves these institutions. *Vice News* shares its status as an American news source with Mitchell, who wrote for a publication still considered at the cutting edge of American journalism. For that reason, I find it appropriate to read the two in connection with one another, extracting where it will be useful, the similarities in how each source positions the gypsies.

But where are the witches? And where did Romania go? I've not yet addressed this text's central subject: gypsy witches in Romania, because I hope to have done analytic justice to introducing the question of gypsyism at large. This text is concerned with how Roma witchcraft operates in contemporary Romania and the similarities it shares with the anecdote Mitchell writes. Specifically, I'm concerned with how Roma witchcraft is framed through *Vice News* in much the same way that traditional gypsyism is framed through Mitchell's profile of Johnny Nikanov. In attempting this, I rely on "Casting Curses and Love Spells with the Most Powerful Witches in Romania," a film produced by *Vice News* that addresses the subject of Roma witchcraft through the eyes of an American publication. I read this film as a literary text that navigates the divide between Roma and Romanian, framed through an American publication concerned with globalization and cosmopolitanism. The following project is inherently literary because I'm concerned with the representations (and misrepresentations) of Roma witches and how these misrepresentations play out in contemporary Romania and American media. I'm concerned, in other words, with assessing these representations exactly as a literary critic is concerned with assessing representations in written text. The fact that much of the work I will do relies on film as my medium of analysis indicates the extent to which Roma witch literature is both young and incomplete, helping me argue that the most productive analysis of Roma witchcraft will also rely on film, which will broaden witches' exposure in today's world.

This book serves three purposes. The first is to contextualize the Roma Witchcraft Movement in contemporary Romania and to articulate how this movement intersects with and diverges from common topics in contemporary witchcraft studies. This will involve a detailed discussion of how Roma witchcraft adopts and uses the figure of the witch as a powerful symbol. The second is to critique the journalism presented in *Vice News* as a publication concerned with broadening the cultural capital of a new generation of media users, primarily millennials. Throughout the text, these two purposes will blend together, and it will often be difficult to separate the two. I've done this deliberately because it's difficult to separate contemporary witchcraft from the medium it must use to extend its reach. The third is to contribute to the young academic project surrounding Roma witchcraft, an underesearched project that represents a niche within contemporary witchcraft studies.

The main argument of this book is that witchcraft is continually involved in a transaction of authority and authorizes a series of three identities that all intersect in the figure of the witch. These identities include: 1. Roma identity, 2. female identity, and 3. capitalist identity. I maintain that the performance of witchcraft allows Roma women to be taken seriously by striking fear into the capitalist mainstream they inhabit. Witchcraft authorizes these identities, and permits Roma women entrance into the European economy, thus authorizing their Roma, female, and capitalist identities. Finally, the medium on which this witchcraft is represented (in my case, *Vice News*) is itself involved in this transaction of authority and authorizes the performance of witchcraft, giving the witches I profile not only a platform to share their practices with the globalized world, but also acknowledging their existence, a move of empowerment that occurs infrequently for the Roma in contemporary Romania.

This argument assumes that our present culture is dealing with a crisis of authority. Many thinkers have pointed this out, arguing from the basis of experts, expertise, and authority.[2] Specifically, I'm concerned with the female Roma community, which according to a report published by the European Roma Rights Centre (ERRC), is seeing an increase in actions designed to disempower and destroy Roma culture (often physically). This includes targeted violence, a "new pattern of police raids systematically conducted in Roma communities" that are coming from "an official institution—the police." Coupled with the fact that unemployment among the Roma is incredibly high ("About 90% of Roma...have an income below the national poverty threshold; about 40% of the children live in households struggling with malnutrition or hunger") this demands a need for explicating the cultural barriers to entering into the mainstream culture and by extension, economy. I present this crisis of authority in contrast to how witchcraft allows Roma communities to combat (or at least, start to combat) these same statistics.

The following three definitions from the *Oxford English Dictionary* help organize what I mean when questioning how witchcraft *authorizes* a thing, identity, action, or person. According to the Dictionary, to authorize can mean: "To vouch for the truth or reality of; to attest." In this respect, witchcraft validates the existence and experience of the Roma in Romania. It furnishes physical, intellectual, spiritual, and literary proof of

---

2   See Nancy Luxon's *Crisis of Authority: Politics, Trust, and Truth-Telling in Freud and Foucault* and Christoper Jenk's "The Crisis of Authority" published in the *New York Times.*

its existence. This will be one of the many times I pause to point out that such a definition is never without bias. To authorize, in other words, always involves a value judgement, an assessment both of validity and effectiveness. Depending on who's arguing and how they're arguing the case, a set of agendas will either make it possible or impossible for the Roma witches to authorize anything. In the spirit of inquiry, I maintain that this is possible.

Authorize can also mean "To give (a person or agent) legal or formal authority (to do something); to give formal permission to; to empower." This definition suggests that measuring the transaction of authority also involves considering the law. This will become significant to my discussion of legislation enacted by the Romanian state on the profession of witchcraft. To authorize, in this respect, signals a legal corroboration, a making valid not only in the eyes of the individual, but also in the eyes of the community with the help of written law. In my case, this will involve fiscal taxation.

Finally, *authorize* can mean "To provide justification or good grounds for (a person) to do something." This definition contributes the third and final shade of meaning to my argument, that when discussing questions of authority and the process of authorizing, we're also concerned with justifying, with giving proof for the actions, identities, and events we support. To authorize, thus, can also mean to supply justification for. Often, this will involve invoking the law, which as the second definition demonstrates, always carries rhetorical weight.

As expected, these three definitions will often blend together. At times, I've done this deliberately, making the argument that it's more useful in the moment to consider the collective rather than the individual. Other times, it will seem unintentional— this, too, makes an argument, for as I will maintain throughout the book, and however hard some avenues of mainstream Romanian culture attempt to do so, it's nearly impossible to separate the Roma from Romanian history. The non-Roma, we will see, have often been placed in charge of writing both groups' histories, which complicates things a good deal.[3]

My argument is inspired by a synthesis of four thinkers whose arguments I quote briefly below. By doing so, I acknowledge not only the extent to which academic traditions are built upon one another, but also the fact that precious little has been written about the Roma witch. I see this book, then, as one of the contributions to a growing sub-heading in witchcraft studies.

Aside from being one of the most comprehensive journal articles on the difference between witchcraft history and identity, Edward Bever's "Witchcraft Prosecutions and the Decline of Magic" also serves as the foundation for addressing why witches are so hated. Bever deconstructs this question through history:

> Prosecutions for witchcraft were relatively rare in Europe before the second half of the 1500s. They involved a combination of scattered trials focusing on individuals suspected of practicing harmful magic and occasional mass trials—mainly in Switzerland and neighboring territories—driven by fear of an underground conspiracy of devil worshippers. In the second half of the century, the number of prosecutions for harmful magic increased, particularly across Northwestern and Central Europe, and routinely led to investigations searching for a diabolic cult. By the early seventeenth century, ordinary people and the governing elite shared a conviction that harmful magic intimated traffic with the devil and participation in an organized cult that threatened the Christian order. Different Europeans emphasized different elements of this belief, with the common people more

---

3   I acknowledge that Roma and non-Roma are clunky categories to invoke. They are, however, the ones most often used in Roma scholarship.

concerned about harmful magic, or maleficium, and the elite more concerned about diabolism. Western Europeans were more likely to view the danger as an integral whole, whereas Eastern Europeans were only beginning to connect local witches and sorcerers to any larger diabolical threat.

Bever outlines the history of witch hating and witch hunting, drawing on H. C. Erik Midelfort, who defines the historical witch trial as a "crisis of confidence." I use *authorize*, then, as a response to "crisis of confidence." This is what I mean by invoking a crisis of authority as the starting point for analyzing the figure of the witch.

Although not explicitly about Eastern European witches, Lisa Bernstein's "Demythifying the Witch's Identity as Social Critique in Maryse Conde's *I, Tituba, Black Witch of Salem*," allowed me to first think about the witch as a discrete identity which could be adopted, traded, discarded, and destroyed. Many of Bernstein's arguments about *I, Tituba* apply to my considerations of Roma witchcraft. The following four passages from Bernstein's article clarify what I mean:

Through her text, Conde redeems the witch figure….

I, Tituba forms part of the writer's continuous struggle to understand individual and collective identities, to place the subject in history, and to link this history to other social and cultural histories….

In constructing a subjectivity for an individual woman who has been 'spoken for' or 'written out' of history, *I, Tituba* challenges dominant historical narratives while problematising its own representational practices.

> [Conde] points out that 'the witch' is a social construct, created to disparage and contain women's powers of healing, of communicating with the unseen world.

In the same way that Bernstein argues that the figure of the witch helps "an individual woman who has been 'spoken for' or 'written out' of history," I will maintain that it also does so for an entire community, the Roma living in contemporary Romania.

Finally, as part of the thrust of my argument will involve discussing how *Vice News* frames witchcraft through film, Helen Berger and Douglas Ezzy's "Mass Media and Religious Identity: A Case Study of Young Witches" provides a compelling foundation for articulating what it means to analyze popular representations of witches, specifically those on screen.

In their writings, Berger and Ezzy evaluate the extent that representations of witches on popular media (films like *The Craft*, *Sabrina the Teenage Witch*, and *Buffy the Vampire Slayer*) affect how young women who identify as witches develop coherent identifies. Although I don't assess the same question, I borrow Berger and Ezzy's insistence that viewing media representations of witchcraft affect an audience. For instance, the two argue, "To a significant extent…positive representations of Witches in the mass media reflect attempts by television producers and filmmakers to continue to engage with the changing interests of young consumers." In slightly different light, I will argue that these deliberate decisions to celebrate witchcraft actually carry political agendas, which for the Romanian state, are designed to empower and disempower the Roma witches. This agenda can be extracted regardless of *Vice News'* intent while filming and publishing its content.

These four thinkers ground my assessment of how witchcraft authorizes Roma identity, female identity, and entrance into the

European economy (capitalist identity). I've done my best to organize these discussions as separate chapters, though content and medium will frequently overlap in the oncoming pages.

My research questions include:

- What issues do the Roma living in Romania face today?

- Why do Roma living in contemporary Romania turn to witchcraft?

- How does the figure of the witch serve to authorize other identities, including but not limited to, the Roma identity, the female identity, and the capitalist identity?

- What truths, illusions, falsehoods, and stereotypes does *Vice News* perpetuate about Roma witchcraft?

- How does reading *Vice News'* film as a literary text affect our understanding of the performativity of witchcraft?

- How does Roma witchcraft implicate the Romanian economy? How can this be read in relation to Silvia Federici's critical writings on the interplay between witchcraft and capitalism?

- How does Roma witchcraft implicate the authenticity and citizenship concerns of the non-Roma?

Chapter 1: Situating the Roma in Contemporary Romania introduces the Roma in contemporary Romania, enumerating their history, and then broaching the subject of Roma witchcraft. I present three lenses through which to analyze Roma history—the historical, mythological, and legislative. These three lenses will become significant to how contemporary Roma identity intersects in the figure of the witch. I also contextualize this information with the challenges the Roma face in today's Romania, demonstrating how advocacy continues to send two-sided messages about the Roma's future.

Chapter 2: Asserting Identity – The Roma Witches outlines the film I analyze in this book, "Casting Curses and Love Spells with the Most Powerful Witches in Romania," directed and produced by *Vice News* and starring Milène Larsson. In this chapter, I summarize the film, placing it in conversation with the notion of performativity. I argue that the Roma witches depicted in the film are forced to perform the roles and actions of traditional witchcraft while blending it with their updated practices as a mechanism to ensure their culture's survival. This involves analyzing the national symbolism and mythology involved in performing witchcraft and evaluating how *Vice News*, as the platform representing this witchcraft, authorizes the presentation. Finally, I evaluate how the interplay of national symbols and mythology, as utilized by the Roma witches, helps them challenge legislation written about them and also helps them establish citizenship within the Romanian state.

Chapter 3: Vice News As Mediator of American Culture picks up where the conversation in the previous chapter leaves off by isolating how *Vice News* serves to authorize Roma identity for a larger audience, the globalized world. I outline the history of *Vice News*, placing it in conversation with three themes I identify in their narrative strategy: the ways they market an insistence on "Under-Reported Stories," the shock value designed for audiences to experience from their films, and how the platform manufactures intrigue in its subjects. In this respect, *Vice News* enters a larger mythology built around the media mogul, while also serving as a mediator of American culture because of how it portrays its subjects. This discussion relies on the notion of hybridity and Marwan Kraidy's "uses-and-gratifications" theory, which together help me argue that part of why *Vice News* is so successful as a mediator of American culture is that it interacts with shocking content that most Americans—specifically millennials—don't have access to (but crave) on an everyday basis. In addition, I address the history that separates Joseph Mitchell's 1942 profile from *Vice News'* 2016 film, using Wicca as a midpoint between the two to help me measure the effects of both Mitchell and *Vice News'* representations of Roma culture. Finally, given this acknowledgement, I address why some Romanians would not respond well to *Vice News'* film about the Roma witches living in Romania.

Chapter 4: Understanding the Roma Witches' Labor Practices addresses how witchcraft authorizes female identity and capitalist identity. In this chapter, I consider the possibilities of the Roma Witchcraft Economy, a thread I discuss in further detail in chapter 5. Specifically, I consider a 2011 tax on Roma witchcraft and practitioners of magic in Romania, and present this tax as a response to male anxiety about female labor and professionalism in Romania. Along with the critical perspective of Alexandra Cotofana, I argue that the Romanian government currently "Governs with magic," an argument Cotofana establishes and I update to include *Vice News*. I then evaluate whether witchcraft, which authorizes female Roma labor, is serving to empower the Roma witches as they participate in capitalist identity. Finally, I isolate how magic, witchcraft, and capitalism intersect in the figure of the Roma witch, and are collectively able to drive legislative policy in contemporary Romania.

Chapter 5: The Roma Witch in Its Xenophobic Socioeconomic Context argues that the tax on witchcraft authorizes capitalist identity by allowing the Roma access to the European economy. This is complicated by the Romanian government who dangles this tax in front of the Roma as a reconciliatory narrative to mend the ways they've previously barred them from participating in the economy. To this end, I discuss how the Romanian government is actually seen to have crafted and gifted the figure of the Roma witch to the Roma people, thus authorizing their existence as a minority group in Romania. This is complicated by evaluating Silvia Federici and Viorel Achim, two scholars whose works I read as a larger conversation on Roma labor. I argue that the Roma are forced to pay a fee for being cultural practitioners of their own, previously-denied heritage and that the Romanian government benefits both fiscally and culturally from this dynamic. Finally, I assert that the Roma should (and will) continue disrupting the European economy through the professionalization of witchcraft because it will allow them to play into the fears of unrepresentative, primarily white male legislators in Romanian government.

History refers both to what really happened and to the reconstruction of what happened; in other words, it is both the past in its objective unfolding and discourse about the past.

—Lucian Boia, *History and Myth in Romanian Consciousness*

We have seen that in practice the magic art may be employed for the benefit either of individuals or of the whole community, and that according as it is directed to one or other of these two objects it may be called private or public magic.

—James Frazer, *The Golden Bough*

Chapter One

SITUATING THE ROMA IN CONTEMPORARY ROMANIA

To many tourists, the country of Romania is typically summarized as a bulleted list of three items: Dracula, Ceaușescu,
and Beautiful Women. These cultural signals are created and
sustained by a powerful, post-Cold War mythology seeking to
simultaneously elevate and undercut the country's status as a
former satellite of the USSR. Even a quick search for Romania
in the *New York Times* reveals a host of articles whose headlines
do little more than extend lackluster representations of the
country: "Romania Names 3rd Prime Minister in a Year Amid
Struggle Over Corruption," "Romania Braces for President's
Decision on Bills Seen as Weakening Judiciary," and most fa-
mously, "Anti-Corruption Protest Draws Tens of Thousands
Across Snowy Romania." These dilute our popular understandings of the genuine struggles this country faces and are often
deployed in an effort to undercut the status of this seemingly
non-competitive European ally. But it's impossible to ignore
(or downgrade) the sociopolitical concerns this country shares
with the remainder of Europe. Among many other pressing
concerns, contemporary Romania faces a difficult battle with

government corruption and an immediate need to integrate the Roma population living inside the country.

The Roma, whose history in Europe extends as far back as 1500 years ago, occupy a distinct space outside mainstream Romania's economic and cultural achievements.[1] They are Otherized, cast as non-productive, non-contributors to the European economy. Yet this group's participation in Romanian culture and by extension the European economy reveals a complex interplay predicated on situating them within a culture that is increasingly working to push them out.

The place of contemporary Romania, I argue, is a result of these dynamic, often contradictory representations of a country that appeals to the outsider because it allows them the privilege of simultaneously reveling in and shaming a place whose historical exoticism hasn't entirely disappeared. Romania presents itself as an appealing alternative to the "politically-correct world" where exercising general cultural insensitivities isn't completely faux pas. It provides a space to exercise these insensitivities at the encouragement of a popular imagination that models this same behavior, bolstered by problematic legislation designed to disempower the Roma while also sending them the signals of reconciliation and redemption they must heed to integrate into the mainstream. These complex dynamics ultimately unite the traveler with the cultural machinations of a country whose tourism industry is created on—even sustained by—these types of experiences. This book isolates the cultural moment produced by Roma witchcraft to define a discrete space where the Roma are allowed and encouraged to practice an authentic, historically denied identity (the Roma witch) while also ana-

---

1   See Elizabeth Mendizabel's scholarship for a more precise presentation of this history.

lyzing the complex dynamics behind the regulation of Roma witchcraft, and the modes required for its survival. The Roma witch presents an opportunity to perform an "illegal identity" within the confines of the supposedly legal superstructure of the government, the ultimate—and only—move of regulated empowerment this group is afforded in the country it inhabits.

Interpretative Frameworks for Defining the Roma

Viorel Achim and the Creation of History

In his monumental analysis of the Roma, *The Roma in Romanian History*, Viorel Achim presents Gypsies as a "population of Indian origin" that has been denied their human rights and enslaved. I quote Achim's analysis at length because it establishes an authoritative underpinning to the contemporary plight of today's Roma.[2]

Achim traces the history of the Roma from the Middle Ages until the 1990s, beginning by asserting that the Roma language, "also known as Romani or Romanes, belongs to the Indo-European language family."[3] He utilizes the Roma's no-

---

2   In the same way that Achim does, I also use the term "Gypsy" in a historical sense and the term "Roma" to represent a contemporary understanding of this group of people. In present-day Romania, however, the slur "Țigan" is used and abused across popular and political culture, by children, adults, and politicians alike.

3   Later, I consider the role language plays in creating national identity through the lens of Lucian Boia, Romania's paramount historian turned mythologist whose *History and Myth in Romanian Consciousness* situates the creation of a Romanian People inside the creation of a Romanian language.

madism as the foundation of his anthropological and sociological analysis of their development and marginalization in Romania history, balancing this by discussing their occupations. He frequently returns to a conclusion he draws about the Roma in medieval Romanian society, a conclusion that is still true today: "In medieval Romanian society, Gypsies had an inferior social status." This gives the historical precedence required to sustain a mythology that continually casts the Gypsy as inferior in all socio-political realms of experience. Later, other thinkers will consider the role mythology plays in the uses and abuses of Romanian history.

Achim then identifies the Gypsy "problem" European politics of 1930s and 1940s—including its bio-politics—is founded on. It is during this latter time that the state mandated "'handbook' for minorities policy'...[included] concepts such as 'ethnic-purity,' 'inferior ethnic groups,' 'ethnic promiscuity,'...[and] 'ballast minorities,'" thus linking the Gypsies as a problem to the culture and the state. Achim concludes, "'The Gypsy problem' was conceived as a racial problem and the solutions proposed were consequently of racial nature.'" These solutions, Achim points out, often included forced haircuts, captive work, and even sterilization in the establishment of the "gradual isolation of the Gypsies in a kind of ghetto." As such, Roma history is incomplete without a keen understanding of the state-sanctioned ways the Roma have been marginalized, displaced, and tortured. This analysis forces us to situate examples of marginalization and physical violence within the legislative ways today's Roma are cast out of Romanian culture.

In "The Gypsies During the Communist Regime," Achim identifies a clear erasure of the Gypsy population from legal life: "From the year 1948, when Communism established itself fully in Romania, the Gypsies no longer appear in official documents of political nature." This complete erasure of the physical, and by extension ethnic existence that the Roma pride themselves on cannot be ignored as we move to understanding their place in present-day Romania. At this moment, the Roma are physically and figuratively denied existence in the law. Yet it must be placed in counterpoint with Achim's stance that "a relatively large number of Gypsies were employed in the Party apparatus, the militia, army and the security apparatus" of Communist Romania. Where does this leave us?

This contradiction is emblematic of the present-day status of the Roma as a simultaneous object of physical revulsion (best identified in the ethnocentric narratives aimed at excluding them from Romania in particular and the EU in general) and as an object of fascination (represented by the resurgence and heavy monetization of Roma witchcraft) which has reached American consciousness through its portrayal in platforms such as *Vice News*, *The New Republic*, and the *New York Times*. Later, Ioana Szeman will have much to say about how this contradiction is hegemonically designed to cast the Roma as Other when it's most convenient to the non-Roma majority. For the purposes of my argument, I add that this contradiction also reveals how witchcraft, for the Roma, is one of the final ways this group of people can assert an authentic, historically-denied identity in the face of a nation aiming to destroy their existence through the marriage of market capitalism and ethno-nationalism.

Lucian Boia and the Creation of Myth

History is a powerful tool for working with the question of the Roma in contemporary Romania. In what follows, I suggest

45

that it's also an incomplete tool for understanding the Roma's interconnected place within nationalist history and myth. It's impossible to situate them accurately, and to honestly contextualize them within Romanian history, if we don't understand how their existence transgresses accepted history—the history, for instance, of Viorel Achim. For this, I turn to mythology and the writing of Lucian Boia, whose *History and Myth in Romanian Consciousness* serves as one of the most authoritative interpretations of the country's history. Without myth, for instance, Joseph Mitchell's profile of Johnny Nikanov reads much more like a trusted confessional rather than a foundational myth deployed for creating stereotypes and national agendas. In adopting this same agenda years later, *Vice News* also transacts with these same stereotypes and national agendas, leading us to question not only the historical veracity of its reporting, but also how it deploys mythology without fully appreciating it. In order to better understand this, we first need to understand mythology's place in Romanian history at large.

Published in 1997, *History and Myth in Romanian Consciousness* accurately and artfully lays the foundation for the literary reading of *Vice News* that I undertake in the oncoming chapters. Appropriately, Boia begins the text with a definition of history: "History refers both to what really happened and to the reconstruction of what happened; in other words, it is both the past in its objective unfolding and discourse about the past." This definition acknowledges mythology's role in history without even needing to name it, putting forth an understanding of history whose relevance is still perceptible today. Myth, on the other hand, is an "imaginary construction (which, once again, does not mean either real or unreal, but arranged according to the logic of the imaginary), which serves to highlight the essence of cosmic and social phenomena, in close relation to the fundamental values of the community, and with the aim of ensuring that community's cohesion." By the "essence of cosmic and social phenomena," Boia circumvents the elephant in the room—History—and downplays this existential figure by refusing to name it. More on this later.

His definition of myth relies on an understanding that myths 1. converge and diverge with a community's goals and 2. aim to ensure a community's "cohesion," thus also raising questions about how myths enforce cohesion through the groups of people they work to keep out. Myths can be communal and empowering, but they can also be limiting and disempowering. This understanding of mythology will become relevant when I consider the Roma's place in creating Romanian national mythology, a subject Boia only roughly sketches.

Boia maintains how "Myth is highly integrative and simplificative, having a tendency to reduce the diversity and complexity of phenomena to one privileged axis of interpretation," thus identifying how myth tends to clash with historical accuracy, which is typically predicated on the same "diversity and complexity" myth elides. But how is Romania implicated in this discussion? Part of the problem in accurately answering this question involves how Boia situates Romania on the outsides of both the Orient and the Occident, in an interstitial *no space*: "The Romanians are neither Western nor Eastern. They lie between these two worlds and can be a unifying bond: We are between the Near and Far East…and the West." What he suggests is that the Romanian people were a people conveniently ahistorical—battling with a history they neither owned nor wanted foisted on them, that of East versus West. Rather, in their need to defend and define a history, the Romanians struggled with "geographical mythology," which required, "geographical predestination, a well-defined space, marked out by clear borders, which has been reserved for them from the beginning." This was never the case for Romania, which as both Achim and Boia demonstrate, struggled to define its borders as much as it struggles today (if it's the goal after all) to define its national identity. Enter myth.

Boia identifies how myth filled this void, blending a "geographical mythology" where there never was one with a "foundational myth" that he admits, Romanians "cannot prevent": "In invoking their origins, the Romanians, like any other people, have the feeling that they are affirming their individuality and defending their rights." These calls for individuality and the "defending [of] rights" substitute for what Boia describes as a nation grappling with the "absence, for a thousand years, of a Romanian state," a singular, unified, European state. It becomes easier to see how a people keenly interested in "affirming their individuality and defending their rights," once given a national image, become more willing—even paranoid—with defending this image from the perceived attacks committed by the Roma, the ultimate markers of a people outside the East and West.[4]

Of the Roma, Boia identifies how, "Many things are blamed on the Gypsies, from the insecurity of everyday life (murders, robberies) to the damaging of the country's image abroad." He goes on to cite, "According to the polls, approximately two-thirds of Romanians do not like Gypsies," but ultimately situates these attitudes as "the result of history, not of any Romanian predisposition," suggesting, in other words, that any country would treat the Roma as the Romanians do, if they knew what Romania were going through; if they shared the same history. Which begs the question, isn't Romania the only

---

4   Later, Ioana Szeman will connect these attacks to the paranoia of defining and policing citizenship—of defining, in other words, who is and isn't legally "Romanian," for what it's worth.

nation that has lived Romanian history? This seems to nullify the argument, and point him in the same direction from where he began. Although the logical fallacy may be excusable, what Boia is attempting to do here is actually to distance himself from the history he wants readers to know he doesn't identify with (Roma history) while affirming the "true and tested" Romanian History he wishes his text to represent.

He ends the discussion on a flat note by concluding that the reason why Roma and non-Roma can't seem to get along is the fault of capital H History: "History shows how difficult it is to harmonize communities of different origins, language, religion, and culture." This is a convenient invocation of History where it suits him best because it allows him to devolve into generalities that can be easily defended. It certainly is difficult to "harmonize communities of different origins, language, religion, and culture," but Boia himself would be the first to point out that history isn't easy.

To Boia, the "history[5] of the Romanians is understood in strictly conflictual terms, as a continuous struggle for ethnic and state survival." One of the conflicts enacted on this stage is that between the Roma and non-Roma, both groups willing and able to engage in and co-opt authentic Romanian mythology to ensure their community's survival. For the non-Roma, this involves invoking nationalist figures such as Vlad Tepes, King Carol I, and King Mihai I which Boia characterizes at impressive length.[6] These are mythological figures who repre-

---

5   Note the lowercase "h" here. Though it seems like I'm making a big deal out of one small linguistic decision, Boia is too comfortable invoking the history of others to satisfy his own without giving due discussion to how Roma history is deeply intertwined with non-Roma history.
6   See chapter 2 of *History and Myth in Romanian Consciousness* for this discussion.

49

sent a concrete, identifiable history that can serve to include and exclude communities who identify or do not identity, who honor or do not honor these figures. This is a strategic invocation of history. On the other hand, for the Roma, this involves engaging with witchcraft as a substitute for these foundational myths, which, even if they did exist, would not be honored by the non-Roma majority. The Roma studied in this text engage with witchcraft because it provides an accessible, highly-marketable, and even profitable avenue to create a material culture they lack but must demonstrate to survive. The performance of witchcraft authorizes their existence as Roma, as women, and as participants in the European economy, a task each of these identities has traditionally been barred from by racism.

Ioana Szeman and the Creation of Citizenship

Thus far, I've addressed two avenues in which the Roma are barred from participation in Romanian culture. The first is strictly historical while the second involves the addition of narrative to history to create myth. The third, then, involves the interplay of these dynamics, plus government legislation. In this section, I consider the role citizenship plays in the creation (or prevented creation) of Roma history and myth. For this, I draw on the research of Ioana Szeman, whose *Staging Citizenship: Roma, Performance and Belonging in EU Romania*, provides one additional interpretative framework for contextualizing the Roma in contemporary Romania.

The thrust of Szeman's argument is that a "citizenship gap" exists between the Roma and non-Roma in contemporary Romania. This citizenship gap is created and sustained by blending problematic representations of Roma in popular culture with government legislation designed to disenfranchise them. For Szeman, "actual citizenship" is the "ability to take advantage of the citizenship rights that have been gained through legal citizenship but which, if 'understood as private 'liberties' or 'choices', are meaningless, especially for the poorest and most disenfranchised, without enabling conditions through which they can be realized." Actual citizenship, in other words, equals legal citizenship plus access to avenues of cultural expression. Because the Roma are seen as Other, they are denied access to avenues of cultural expression and acceptance; for Szeman, this denial is enacted through a "not us" gesturing that non-Roma use to keep Roma out of culture: "Roma in Romania are jettisoned as 'not us', a gesture that maintains the citizenship gap at the social and discursive levels for Roma, and the privilege of the majority through monoethnic paradigms of nation and citizenship." That Romanian Culture is invoked to enact this "not us" gesturing is significant for it brings the support of thousands of years of narrative and myth with it. As Lucian Boia demonstrates, it's difficult to identify just what is meant by invoking the place of Romanian Culture, but its effects are always clear.

Szeman maintains that Roma are forced into "performing civility" in order to access a few of the many avenues of cultural expression afforded by contemporary Romanian life. This is the performative aspect she identifies in her text, arguing that the Roma counteract the "not us" gesturing by performing respectability politics. (This will become critical to my discussion of Roma witchcraft, one of the avenues I present as a counterpoint to the "not us" gesturing the Roma experience.) I argue that Roma witches are able to counteract the "not us" gesturing by performing—here I rely on Szeman's use of the term—the identity of the Roma witch. Although this identity is not accepted by the mainstream non-Roma, it allows the Roma to partially transcend the extent to which they've been barred from participating in Romanian culture just enough so that they can survive (and thrive) financially, while also asserting a distinct identity. I see this identity, then, as an answer to the "not us" gesturing they encounter daily. In this respect, witchcraft also authorizes citizenship, allowing Roma women to experience what it means to have "actual citizenship" by performing a cultural identity that only belongs to them.

Although Szeman doesn't discuss Roma witchcraft, she maintains two avenues of cultural expression that *are* afforded to the Roma in contemporary Romania. The first is gypsy television, while the second is *manele*, or Roma folk music. Although it seems odd to connect television, music, and witchcraft, these three avenues share the notion of performativity at their core, which I argue is essential to the survival of Roma witchcraft, a highly ritualized, highly stylized expression of culture:

> While there are many debates around the origin and ownership of folk music, there is less controversy, in Romania at least, about whom manele belongs to: it belongs to the Țigani. This hugely successful and controversial music genre is played almost exclusively by Roma in Romania; unlike in other countries, where genres such as turbo-folk are sung and controlled by non-Roma, in Romania it is Roma who run the manele market. Successful music entrepreneurs such as Dan Bursuc, and manele singers such as Florin Salam and Nicolae Guță, have gained a privileged position in Romania through music; but they are far from being accepted as full citizens and part of the nation and, in fact, Roma musicians' almost complete control of the manele genre in Romania makes the music less acceptable. Tolerated because of their financial success, these musicians are often seen as examples of market corruption, rather than of talent and hard work.

Manele, or Roma folk music, is thus seen as a way to create citizenship for the Roma, to manufacture political status out of an expression of culture that is primarily dominated by the Roma. At the same time, however, Szeman quickly points out that one of the main reasons *manele* is tolerated is that its musicians experience great "financial success." This example suggests that even if they're in charge of creating their own material culture, the Roma are still scrutinized and infrequently accepted as participants in contemporary Romanian culture:

> Manele thus splinters the Romanian public along status and ethnic lines as well as East–West vectors. This places Roma musicians at the crux of debates in Romania about identity, Europe and the 'Orient', modernity and tradition, all of which are epitomized by criticism or praise of manele.

As the figure of the Roma witch will do, *manele* musicians are constantly forced to defend an avenue of cultural expression from scrutiny, non-acceptance, and even corruption. As Szeman demonstrates, this debate splinters around ethnic and socioeconomic lines, leading us to believe that music, a communal activity after all, is doing more to alienate than to bring together.

The same dynamics are present in what Szeman refers to as "Gypsy Television," or soap operas featuring Roma actors: "While the soaps represented the beginning of a wave of Romanian TV programmes featuring Roma characters played by non-Roma, Roma had long been among the most popular entertainers in the Romanian music industry." Szeman quickly criticizes these soaps, however, for forcing non-Roma actors to perform Roma identity—to perform, in other words, the respectability Roma citizens are forced to engage in on a daily basis: Roma actors are portrayed speaking "extravagant and/or ungrammatical [Romanian]," and are deeply "[obsessed] with

Roma wealth within the post-socialist media's overall focus on excessive consumption." Szeman writes, "Their broken accents—stereotypical of Roma speaking Romanian—and their ghetto-fabulous garb, with bling and unorthodox mixtures of traditional costume and urban clothing, made them the soaps' most picturesque and most popular characters," while also undercutting any credibility afforded to the Roma community as a result of this performance. Since non-Roma actors are cast to represent the Roma experience, the Roma do not benefit from this avenue of cultural expression. They cannot even act for themselves.

It's important to note that the soaps are criticized for the half-hearted, often politically incorrect exposure they give the Roma: "On blogs and in online comments about the soaps, some non-Roma audience members alleged that the 'racism' of the Roma/Gypsy characters encouraged anti-Romanian racism and was a threat to a nation that was already Gypsified." But as is often the case, the *we can't please everyone* argument conveniently hides racist insecurities about acceptance and citizenship. Whereas the gypsy soaps are designed as a pathway to create actual citizenship, what remains is a cultural signal in the dark, an expression of Roma culture that ultimately falls victim to the whims of market capitalism, obsessive advertising, and tone deafness.

I rely on Szeman's notion of "performing civility," though diverge with her conclusion that this performance is entirely negative. Whereas she "theorize[s] [that performance leads to] the racialization of Roma...[and] their misrecognition in everyday life, onstage and in media representations," I'm primarily concerned with how this performance allows Roma witches to define a sustained, articulated culture in the face of a mainstream culture that's increasingly working to push them out.

What's more, I argue the Roma actually acknowledge their own stereotyping and act strategically so as to benefit from their misrepresentation. This is achieved through the figure of the witch, introduced later in this chapter. Although this cultural performance does indeed lead to "misrecognition in everyday life, onstage and in media representations," as Szeman argues, it's also, in the case of the Roma witches, deeply important to the definition of a material culture that's bought into the figure of contemporary witchcraft.

The Issues They Face

Today, an estimated 621,600 Roma live in Romania, a figure well within an estimate that is probably closer, scientists acknowledge, to 1 million. Achim details how "The majority of the Roma live well below the standards of civilization common to the rural or urban locality in which they reside." Although the distinction between the linguistic categories of Gypsy and Roma is clear in the academic literature, this is not the case in popular culture, where newspapers and politicians alike repeatedly demonize this group by presenting them as Others and even encouraging the mainstream culture to do the same.

In response, groups like the European Roma Rights Center (ERRC) have become more popular in Romanian consciousness. This group self-identifies as a "Roma-led international public interest law organization working to combat anti-Romani racism and human rights abuse of Roma through strategic litigation, research and policy development, advocacy and human rights education." Although this mission statement appears to clearly assert an empowered identity, I must note that this group is committed to something that is not popular across much of Romania, or the EU for that matter. What's more, the proliferation of diverse, complex conflicts within the Roma group itself do not help its cause in the public's eye. These dynamics, which are deliberately used to demonize the Roma against their own identities, are incapsulated in a comment made by Madalin Voicu, a parliamentarian in the Romanian government, whose disparaging remarks became famous in 2002:

> Our gypsies are stupid. They could at least be crafty but they aren't. They are just primitives and they manage to irritate the entire society which is already watching them closely....They run through the country and Europe barefoot, slimy and dirty, wearing clothes which are more likely to disgust you than make you feel sorry for them....Begging, soliciting and being disorganized will never bring them any advantages.

This statement clearly asserts an ethnic nationalism on behalf of the Romanian government, but this conclusion is complicated by the fact that Voicu himself is a Roma politician who has also enjoyed a successful tenure as the conductor of the Bucharest Symphony Orchestra and a member of the Social Democratic Party. These contrasts and unsuspecting reversals afflict much of the Roma advocacy discourse, which often undercuts its own ethos by positioning itself as a confused group signalizing toward a productive future but still somewhat uncertain of how to get there. Voicu's insistence on craftiness will become important to how Roma witches actually use their own stereotyping to their advantage. One cannot help but connect this to the gypsy soaps Szeman discusses, which serve as productive attempts at defining a material culture for the Roma, but ultimately fail in the work they do to honestly cast and represent Roma culture for the non-Roma mainstream. In response, some Roma women turn to witchcraft as an identity that helps them legitimate their existence in the mainstream.

This is not to say that governing bodies refuse to help the Roma. Organizations like the European Commission (EC) do develop advocacy and improve the Roma's immediate living conditions in Europe. According to the EC's Report "Roma Integration in Romania," they claim that of the €22.9 billion in EU funds Romania will receive, "at least 30.8% will be spent on the ESF, with at least 20% of that going towards the promotion of social inclusion and combating poverty. The latter amount could also finance Roma-related measures." Inside a culture predicated on government corruption, however, it isn't difficult to see how many of these funds could disappear in other directions or be misused against the Roma as most of their accountability measures reside primarily in the ERCC, an advocacy group which is ridiculed and not taken seriously by many Europeans who still envision them through the Achim's fated "Gypsy problem."

High levels of government corruption also complicate this dynamic. During the December 2017 protests in Bucharest, which were extensively covered by the *New York Times*, over 500,000 people gathered to protest new legislation that "makes it harder to prosecute high-level corruption crimes": "Those gathered in Bucharest chanted anticorruption slogans, denounced the current government and called for early elections, according to several local reports." This political affinity is laudable, especially in a post-Soviet bloc country still clouded by the legacy of Ceaușescu's stifling regime, but nowhere does it include—or mention for that matter—the Roma and their concerns. Throughout contemporary consciousness, the Roma are deliberately absented from the sociopolitical sphere in an effort to silence their intimately Romanian history. As such, I position the Roma as a group operating within a context of governmental corruption they simultaneously understand and are forced to accept partial blame for. As scapegoats, they are repeatedly demonized as a burden to the European economy. I will have more to say about this in chapter 3, which positions Roma witchcraft as an outlet for enacting revenge against the mainstream, which continually scapegoats the Roma for the economic problems Romania—and much of the EU faces—while barring their entry into the economy.

The competition to "integrate the Roma community within Romanian society," as one *Economist* writer puts it, forces the realization that the Roma writ large are being socialized into a culture that largely rejects them—yet simultaneously sends them messages urging (even demonizing) them for not joining the mainstream culture. This socialization, in turn, has forced the Roma to embrace the few professions still afforded to them. One of these professions is Roma witchcraft.

In this respect, the Roma are a group who have been written into history by a polyphony of voices, some productive, others destructive. Although it's difficult to fault the work completed by historians like Viorel Achim, these efforts are one of few to write Roma history in honest, productive light. All too often, their history falls victim to voices such as Madalin Voicu and followers of anti-Roma propaganda. One faces the challenge of integrating Achim's history of the Roma within the all-powerful myths established by Lucian Boia and the concerns enumerated by Ioana Szeman. In fact, Szeman's notion that the Roma's many problems today are a result of the "citizenship gap" they experience helps us understand the statistics cited in this section. What, then, can we make of the fact that even the Romanian government is responsible for sending these destructive signals?

In what follows, I suggest that this has always been historically true for the Roma and will continue being true unless more deliberate measures are taken to ensure that they're allowed to create their own history. Unfortunately, as I demonstrate, this is not happening since popular news media outlets including *Vice News* are capitalizing on creating history, myth, and citizenship to extend clouded messages about the future of *their* Roma in contemporary Romania.

Problematizing the Witch

Where is the witch? And, where has she been hiding? In a book about witchcraft, I've said precious little about this figure. One way to reconcile this is that she's been here all along. The proverb, "Wherever the gypsies go, there the witches are, we know!" illustrates this sentiment, for the figure of the witch has always been associated with gypsy culture. According to one scholar, "Gypsies have always been associated with magic and witchcraft" and were "frequently accused of theft, witchcraft, and child abduction."

Another way involves the creative license I've taken in first presenting the gypsy and then the witch. It would be difficult to argue that either of these identities does not create overwhelming associations in every reader's mind—that these constellations are rich and often laden with memories and anecdotes, like the ones presented in the preface; that these memories and anecdotes, in turn, deeply alter the course of our thoughts and imaginings about these two figures. For the purposes of my argument, these associations are designed to damage rather than empower. For both the gypsy and the witch, these associations are only now turning to more productive light, in arguments designed to give honest exposure to both communities. I've withheld discussing the figure of the witch until now in order to streamline our considerations of the Roma first and the witch second. This has allowed me considerable creative liberty in presenting a set of three lenses through which we can analyze the Roma and the witch—the historical, the mythological, and the legislative. As is always the case, it's much more difficult to answer the question of which came first, the gypsy or the witch, than it is to ask it. I suspend that question in favor of another, *Why the witch?*

The witch, Kristen Sollée tells us, is "having a moment":

> Film and television are filled with tales of witches and otherworldly women, visual art and literature are plumbing the depths of pagan lore, and runaways are replete with occult symbolism. For the newly anointed 'generation witch,' empowerment is central to her appeal.

After its publication in 2017, Sollée's *Witches, Sluts, Feminists: Conjuring the Sex Positive*, raised a pop cultural firestorm, spawning articles with titles such as: "Are Witches the Ultimate Feminists?", "Witch Kids of Instagram", and "The Witch Continues to Enchant as a Feminist Symbol" arriving on publications including *The Guardian*, *The Baffler*, and the *New York Times*. If that didn't inspire us enough to take them seriously, witches have also taken over Instagram and Tumblr.[7]

According to Kate Guadagnino of the *New York Times*, the witch continues to be a relevant feminist symbol because it resists "the ongoing commercialization of feminism" and is "not so easily corrupted, retaining both an earthiness and a hard-

---

[7]   See Antonia Blumberg's article in *The Huffington Post* titled "15 Instagram Accounts All Witches, Healers, And Goddess-Lovers Should Follow." Clearly, the witch *is* "having a moment."

ness, one born of an instinct for self-preservation." Along with Sollée, Guadagnino makes the point that although the connection between witchcraft and feminism is a relatively new invention of third wave feminism, it's easy to manage: the witch has always been a symbol of the persecuted minority. Feminism, in turn, provides ways for reclaiming that identity—for doing something that would have been unheard of during the European witch hunt: proudly, unabashedly calling oneself a witch. The witches addressed in this book begin by proudly—at times even irritatingly—making this reclamation not only to themselves and the interviewer who follows them, but also to their audience, provided by *Vice News*. These women use witchcraft to authorize their existence as female practitioners of a historically-denied culture. By allying themselves with the historical mysteriousness of witchcraft, the Roma witches use witchcraft in order to be taken seriously—to be authorized in the eyes of the predominantly white mainstream.

Laurie Penny picks up this same argument, writing that "The craze for witchery displays an encouragingly wide understanding that for social change to happen someone has to feel threatened" and distinctly locates Instagram's granting of a platform for online witchcraft in social activism, a highly marketable dynamic that appeals to many millennials on the platform:

> Traditionally, witches did not do magic in order to rule the world, or damn it. Witches worked in their communities for the common good, as well as their own. Witches took control of their own destinies and helped others do the same—and there's danger whenever a woman decides to do that, whatever the cost, no matter what she calls it. The magic might not be 'real'—but it works anyway.

Repeatedly, these arguments return to using the figure of the witch as a mode of empowerment—for young girls, for women, for us all. The witches I will discuss tow the line between using their magic "in order to rule the world" or their particular place in the world," and committing "common good." At times, they will diverge from "common good" and actively use their powers for what they perceive is evil, but even this is done for a reason.

The *Guardian* writer who first reviews Sollée's book echoes the sentiment of the previous two articles, asking the pertinent question, "Are witches the ultimate feminists?" In the increasingly commercialized global culture we inhabit, the witch serves not only as a unifying symbol of female empowerment, but also a reclamation of a time when women were thought dangerous. He/she/they may very well be the "ultimate feminist," but as others have pointed out, only time will tell. Why, then, do I choose to focus on only one witch family?

In the chapters that follow, I discuss the Mincas, a Roma witch family living in Romania portrayed by *Vice News*. I consider the film a piece of literature because its first and foremost concern is representation—representing the Roma witch on screen through the platform of *Vice News*. I read this film as literature in order to acknowledge how the history it depicts is inherently literary—that is, it involves the same lenses I introduce in this chapter, those of history, mythology, and legislation. It is through the knitting together of these three separate lenses that the Roma witch identity is built and positioned in response to the non-Roma mainstream. At times this is done honestly; at times maliciously. This allows me to deconstruct both what is said in the documentaries and how it's framed, presenting not only a reading of the Minca witches, but also a critique of how *Vice News* represents them. I do this rather than address witchcraft writ large because doing so would require a volume of writing beyond my present scope. This is not a book about witchcraft in general. Furthermore, I'm concerned with

Roma witchcraft, a specific—even hyper-specific—category of witchcraft that converges and diverges with important traits of witchcraft writ large. That being said, I will repeatedly return to the interpretative frameworks outlined in this chapter to connect the figure of the Roma witch with witchcraft in general, arguing as I do, that it becomes difficult—at times impossible—to separate the Roma from the witch and the witch from the Roma.

While witch accusers knew how to wield the word, witches themselves were also thought to use language that would betray their aptitude for wickedness. In many trials, evidence was brought forth of an accused witch muttering something under her breath, saying something strangely, or speaking with erudition beyond her station.

—Kristen Sollée, *Witches, Sluts, Feminists: Conjuring the Sex Positive*

If language can be used to suppress dissent against arbitrary and abusive authority—and to name and vilify outsiders—then perverting and reclaiming language can be used to challenge those very systems of oppression. You can't take words out of the mouths of oppressors, but you can subvert the intended meaning of their words.

—Kristen Sollée, *Witches, Sluts, Feminists: Conjuring the Sex Positive*

Chapter Two

"Casting Curses and Love Spells with the Most Powerful Witches in Romania"

As a group already denied the rights and many of the possibilities to assert an authentic identity inside Romania, the Roma have been forced into a cultural dilemma: attempt to answer an identity and then be punished (either through tax or physical and intellectual violence) or dissolve into the background of Romanian society and remain absent. Many (if not all) Roma identities are created *on their behalf*, by a larger Romanian consciousness that continually stifles their authentic culture in favor of debasing them through stereotypes. As the previous chapter demonstrates, the Roma are physically, psychologically, and economically isolated from mainstream Romanian society, even if they're expected to be competitive members of its market economy.[1] This peculiar cultural moment deserves further

---

1   Anti-Roma propaganda often frames the Roma as lazy, non-contributors to Romania's economy (see Voicu's comment cited in the previous chapter).

attention because underneath the ethno-nationalist discourse against the Roma lies a distinct, reactionary, freestyle and free-lance culture the Roma have been forced to inhabit.

Inside this culture, Roma professions such as the gypsy witch appear and are ultimately made visible for the mainstream society. This move demonstrates a sidelining effect, which is detrimental to both the Roma and the mainstream because it places the Roma as a simultaneous object of physical revulsion and object of fascination toyed with at the whims of an increasingly corrupt market capitalism. This market capitalism, and the profit motive more specifically, contribute to the physical destruction of a witchcraft culture predicated on asserting a previously-denied, isolated identity. The final goal for the Roma, it seems, is to accurately and authentically express this reactionary identity, within the limits of an unaccepting mainstream culture that, at any moment, may kick them out.

Vice's 2016 film "Casting Curses and Love Spells with the Most Powerful Witches in Romania" serves as my source material for the investigation of present-day Roma witchcraft that I undertake in this text.[2] In what follows, I summarize the main action in the film before performing a reading of the film's portrayal of witchcraft and how this portrayal is framed through the outlet that is *Vice News*. I've included direct images from the film to help the reader understand the world I'm interacting with here, a complex world based on a literary and mythological history that's not immediately obvious to *Vice News'* intended audience.

---

2   I can attest to the accuracy of this documentary's translation. It is impressive translating work because the dialect of Romanian the Minca family (and other Roma from the documentary) speak frequently drops auxiliary verbs between phrases and relies on heavily contextual knowledge of the conversation being had to develop its meaning.

In its typical first-hand narrative style, this *Vice* film begins with interviewer Milène Larsson arriving in Romania and establishing the subject of her dramatic quest: to interact with and learn from Romania's most famous Roma witch, Mihaela Minca and her family, which is well-known across the country and Europe at large for their "family witch business," to use Larsson's words. Larsson arrives on the scene, meets with her dramatic subject (we are led to believe, for the first time as Minca opens the door for Larsson), and does her best to socialize herself into the world of the witches (fig. 4, 7, and 8).

We quickly learn that Minca and her family are herbalists, who "Collected occult traditions and mixed them with their Orthodox faith." As we're socialized into the world of their town of Mogoșoaia, just north of Bucharest, Minca shares a great deal of valuable material about Roma witchcraft, including its insistence on matrilineal legacy: "Witches' magical power is passed down from mother to daughter." We're also shown a great deal of witch iconography, including brooms, tarot cards, and a cauldron fire that has been prepared for the mock witches' sabbath that begins the film (fig. 2, 3, 4, and 6). These images frame the rest of the film, converging and diverging with the audience's expectations in interesting ways.

The main professional goal of the Minca's witchcraft is to cure love sicknesses: "Suferința de dragoste este cea mai gravă afecțiune de pe pământ. Am poțiuni care îi ajută pe oameni să înceteze suferința" ("Suffering from love is like the worst disease on earth. I have potions that help people stop suffering.") Larsson quickly agrees, sharing how her personal experience with love sickness has deeply disturbed her in the past, demonstrating empathy with the witches' actions. We also learn the philosophy of the Roma witches, artfully and succinctly articulated in Minca's comment at the beginning of the film that

"Am practicat și magia albă, și magia neagră ca o moară bună care mănâncă totul. Vindec bolile copiilor. Îi eliberez pe bărbați din vrăji, fac și căsătorește căsnicia. Asta fac eu pentru că sunt vrăjitoare." ("I practice both white and black magic like a good mill that grinds everything. I cure children's diseases. I release men from love spells, I make and break marriages. That's what I do because I'm a witch.") The logical marker "because I'm a witch" will become relevant to how Minca and the other witches invoke the profession of witchcraft to demonstrate first their existence and legitimacy and then their economic stability. For now, this comment serves as one of the many instances in which the figure of the witch is invoked as a feminist symbol, as a justification for what Sollée identifies when she writes, "the witch is increasingly viewed as a symbol of female power, but she is equally a symbol of female persecution."

As the film continues, we follow Larsson as she is dramatically re-fashioned, the clothes she begins the film in swapped with more appropriate, witch attire (fig. 9). This sartorial decision *authorizes* her in the eyes of the other Roma women, and is seen as a tacit acknowledgement that she's now traded places—physically, symbolically—to become a Roma witch. She then participates in the preparation of an herbal spell (fig. 10) with Minca and her daughter. Later, she meets and interacts with Bratara Buzea, known in the film as "one of the most powerful witches in the world" (fig. 13), and listens as Buzea shares her story of being arrested for practicing witchcraft during Ceaușescu's regime. Finally, Larsson interviews Alin Popoviciu, MP of Democratic Liberal Party, who introduces a segment of the film related to analyzing the laws that regulate witchcraft (fig. 16). Popoviciu alludes to a 2011 law that attempted to tax the profits made by witches and other figures operating in the occult community, but ultimately concludes that the law was not passed because his colleagues were afraid they would be hexed by the witches. This moment will become critical to my connection between licit and illicit forms of magic, along with the role legislation and taxation plays in defining these forms of magic.

The film ends with Larsson's first-hand monologue, summarizing her trip as she stands outside of Minca's house in the street: "One thing is for sure, witches do exist, just like in the fairy tales. And, whether you believe in magic or witchcraft or not is up to you, but whatever you believe will have power over you."

Performing Witchcraft

In this film, the witches' portrayal is highly self-aware and self-referential. This detail is implicated in the concerns of market capitalism the Minca family operates in. One of their primary goals, they reveal early on, is to sustain themselves through profits made by the "family witch business." Given this complication, it's impossible to proceed without acknowledging that Minca is putting on the show that is Roma witchcraft—a complex, dynamic show that's not only required for the performative role she plays as a part of the *Vice News'* film but also mandatory to ensure this culture's survival inside a larger, hegemonic mainstream Romania. In this section, I argue that this self-referential performance is necessary to establish, define, and sustain Roma witch culture because it allows the witches to perform an aspect of "civility" to use Szeman's term, and thus validates their citizenship status within their community. This performance authorizes a series of identities and actions, including their identities as Roma women.

To start, we must consider the fact that, with the aid of *Vice News* as their platform, what the Minca family is doing in this film is putting on a complex, ritualized performance of witchcraft. Yes, they act as the witches they claim to be, but the extent that theatricality plays in this performance should be studied. They are performing their roles—some self-assigned, others traditionally-assigned, and thus enter an accepted vein of the witchcraft tradition. Aside from the fact that this would have been unheard of throughout witchcraft's history where any self-aggrandizing performance was often enough to send witches to their graves, the Minca witches' performance suggests that they're comfortable enough with their roles in this culture to share this performance with Larsson and the crew of *Vice News*.

First, it will be helpful to define these roles before suggesting that the three women must *perform* witchcraft. Then, I'll address the purpose of this performance. Mihaela Minca, known affectionately as "Romania's most powerful witch" (fig. 15), is the leader of the Minca witches. She is in charge of their deliberations, and at times, is even framed so as to appear as being in charge of the film, as, for instance, when she refuses to name a direct price for what she charges for a typical consultation. Her seriousness is a prominent personality trait, defining not only the stories she's willing to share about the witch business and those she withholds, but also how she performs her role as leader of the witches.

Bratara Buzea, known by hearsay as "one of the most powerful witches in the world," is older than Minca, and is defined by the humor she shares with the audience. Unlike Minca, she shares all the details of her role as one of Romania's self-appointed most important witches, and even shares the anecdote of being jailed for practicing witchcraft during Ceaușescu's communist regime (fig. 13). Although Buzea is by no means in charge of the action in the film, and is very much at the whims of Larsson who interacts with her and shares in the moments of comedy she provides, the literary purpose of Buzea's character is to suggest that a lineage of witchcraft exists in Romania. She is both the oldest and most famous (for her generation) and is set in counterpoint with Minca, who is younger and much more profitable. Buzea's lineage is significant to Minca, specifically, who becomes famous because she's part of a witch dynasty. Larsson tells us: "It's this alliance of witch dynasties that makes Mihaela's family one of the most regarded in the country." Even Minca's husband, who is only shown in a brief three-second clip, is part of this dynasty: "El aparține unei familii de vrăjitoare, și eu vin dintr-o familie de vrăjitoare." ("He belongs to a family of witches, and I come from a family of witches, too.") This legacy lends credibility to Roma history. I will have more to say about this dynamic when considering the economics of the witchcraft they engage in.

Finally, although not a witch for the purposes of my argument, Milène Larsson should also be included in the lineup because she serves as the voice of *Vice News* in the film. Through Larsson, we not only learn about the Minca witches, but also experience the witchcraft they perform through Larsson's willingness to participate in their sabbath, curse spells, and deliberations. According to her website, Larsson, is "an award-winning, seasoned international news, current affairs and documentary producer/director/reporter with a decade of experience." She has "made more than 50 films in 20 countries covering issues spanning from the environment and civil rights, to LGBTQI issues, culture, travel and migration, which she has reported on extensively in the British Media Awards." For *Vice News*, specifically, she was a "part of the core team behind *Vice News—Vice's* award-winning news vertical catering to a global youth audience with immersive reports from around the world. She has appeared on HBO, CNN, BBC, Al Jazeera, MSNBC and Sky News, and helped produce '*Vice*' on HBO, an Emmy nominated news-magazine show." She has even spoken at TED, giving a 2017 talk titled "Do we need borders to define our identity?" which draws upon her experience as an international journalist. According to her website, she has participated in nine films, one of which is the 2016 "Casting Curses and Love Spells with the Most Powerful Witches in Romania."

Just how does the witches' theatricality play out? Consider, first, the performative language they use while speaking with Larsson. For example, while boiling herbs for a potion designed to cure love sickness, Minca exclaims, "Sapa va ieși din ele și vom face o poțiune *chiar in fa a ta!*" ("The sap will come out of them and we will make a potion *right in front of you!*"). This moment is self-aware and self-referential because Minca is deliberately making known something that Larsson only timidly asks about: will the potion have any effect on its subject? This self-awareness and self-referentiality is a survival mechanism for the Minca family in particular because it allows them to define the witchcraft tradition they're operating in while also signaling for support from the Roma community in general. They are aware, in other words, that what they say and how they perform it will not only affect the reception they receive as a result of the film, but also the reception the entire Roma community will receive. In this respect, they're tasked, as so many minority groups are, with speaking for their entire culture.

Lorely French suggests that for the Roma, performative storytelling is a "sustenance" to life's difficult moments: "who better to know about the power of storytelling as a source of hope than the Roma,...who, having faced centuries of ostracism and persecution, have developed a vast repertoire of stories from their historically oral culture and thereby increased their chances of survival." In this light, storytelling is a survival mechanism for Minca, who's eager to share her spell with Larsson and the film crew. But it also allows her to ensure that her culture survives, arguing much like French does, that cultures survive through their ability to create and trade aural stories.

This example also allows Minca to interact with the common stereotype that Roma women speak imperfect Romanian, a point Ioana Szeman alludes to when describing Roma speech patterns on television: "[these] broken accents [are…] stereotypical of Roma speaking Romanian[s]." Although this point contributes to Szeman's larger discussion of *manele* (gypsy soaps), and how non-Roma actors are often cast to play Roma parts, it also supports the assertion that what the Minca witches are doing when they engage in self-referential, theatrical speech, is also interacting—and disproving—the stereotype that Roma women speak imperfect Romanian. In this light, the fact that the witches are forced to speak for their entire culture is now productive because it allows them to challenge a commonly held belief about their community that has extensively damaged their reputation in the eyes of the Romanian public. Language, thus, is seen as one of the stages where the battle for acceptance and actual citizenship, to use Szeman's words, is played out. In the context of *Vice News*, which serves as the platform for this political signalizing, this is critical to the Minca witches because it allows them to challenge stereotypes about the Roma while also implicating language as a marker of citizenship—suggesting, ultimately, that they *can* speak grammatically correct Romanian, while also being Roma, while also practicing a witchcraft that now marks them as legal citizens rather than outsiders. This action starts bridging the gap Szeman identifies between legal citizenship and actual citizenship.

Another family witch, Bratara Buzea, shares an anecdote of how witchcraft operated under Ceaușescu's regime; her speech pattern follows these same performative qualities: "Sub Ceaușescu nu ne-a fost permis să practicăm vrăjitoria. Am făcut totul în secret. Am fost urmărit și trimis în închisoare. Nu m-am speriat. L-am bătut, polițistul. L-am luat și l-am bătut. Vroia să-mi ia banii, cărțile de tarot, dar nu putea. Am slujit șase luni în închisoare și apoi am venit acasă." ("Under Ceaușescu we weren't allowed to practice witchcraft. We would do everything secretly. I was tracked down and sent to prison. I wasn't scared. I beat him up, the policeman. I took the bat and beat him up. He wanted to take my money, my tarot cards, but he couldn't. I served six months in prison and then came home").[3] Whereas an American audience may rationalize these details as slapstick comedy, this neglects the larger cultural conclusion that the comedy we derive from Bratara Buzea's seemingly fearless encounter with the police is not emblematic of all Roma interactions with law enforcement, let alone those interactions under Ceaușescu's regime. Recall Achim, who details how under communism, the Roma were first erased from existence when, in 1948, they "no longer appeared in official documents of political nature." Although a "relatively large number of Gypsies were employed in the Party apparatus," this was primarily done "not so much under the aegis of the policy of promoting national minorities…

---

3   Ceaușescu's fear of witchcraft, along with some of his other personality ticks, are best represented in Ion Pacepa's 1987 *Red Horizons: The True Story of Nicolae and Elena Ceau escu's Crimes, Lifestyles, and Corruption*. Unfortunately, the book's veracity itself is often called into question as Pacepa was a three-star general who floated in and out of Ceaușescu's inner circle.

but, rather in the conditions of the Communist regime's social policy, which aimed at…destroying the old social structure that was unwilling to accept the new order."The systemic erasure of Roma nationality clearly began before Ceaușescu, an assertion that challenges any humor the audience is intended to extract from *Vice's* film.

What's more, the legislatively expressed attitude toward the Roma during the Communist regime was historically "based on the cultural and ethnic assimilation of the Gypsies, considering that they can only be 'civilized' if they give up their cultural heritage and become 'Romanians' or 'Hungarians.'" Of course, this leads one to question whether we have made little— if any—progress in extending the rights and responsibilities of a contemporary global state to the present-day Roma. After all, Minca probably practiced witchcraft during the communist period as a way to ensure her family's economic stability. Placed in counterpoint with the EC report cited in chapter 4, which lauds the perceived progress of impressive healthcare and education advances for the Roma, Achim's analysis of progress rings hollow, underwhelming at best, and the result of downright criminal negligence at worst. It's unsurprising, then, that Minca presents and performs her character to the extent that she does. Ultimately, it reveals a troubling undercurrent of negligence once we realize that the Roma are still struggling to integrate into mainstream Romania. Yet the economic opportunities afforded to Roma are seldom enough to sustain their existence inside the economic pressures of the twenty-first century marketplace.

This same dynamic is also evident in Minca's choice of style, as, for example, when she explains that it's important to wear bright clothes when performing witchcraft because "când port haine strălucitoare, răspândesc fericirea, dragostea și frumusețea." ("when I wear shiny clothes I spread happiness, love, and beauty.") Even more, critical, however, is the garment she wears: an IA, or traditional Romanian blouse. It would be difficult to overstate the significance of this decision, especially in a country that so values symbols of national unity adorned on women's bodies.

In Romania, the IA is implicated in everything from national events, social gatherings, and school pride. Academic articles have even been published about this symbol. Ioana Corduneanu and Nicolae-Sorin Dragan's "Semiotics of White Spaces on the Romanian Traditional Blouse, the IA" is one addition to a rich cultural discussion surrounding this garment. For these scholars, the IA is "a plea for the (re)vitalisation of folk traditions, in particular the manufacturing techniques of the shirt with a crinkled neckline, or the shirt with embroidery (shirt with '*altita*'), as the Romanian blouse is known." One way to read these "folk traditions" is as a return to the folkloric roots of Roma witchcraft.

By "understanding clothes as a system of signs in relation to other systems of social signs," they perform a critical reading of the IA, going so far as to argue, in the style of Levi-Strauss and Roland Barthes, that:

> We understand the Romanian blouse as a language also from the viewpoint of rules to generate this cultural object. This entire sequential order of making the object (the Romanian blouse, IA), from rules of weaving to rules of cutting fabric and embroidering (sewing) our ancient motifs on fabric configure the 'grammar' of a language. We know that the presence of a rule 'potentially leads to an unlimited number of applications.'

Their reading is impressive, paying special attention to how everything from learning the stitch patterns required to navigating the white spaces on the blouse holds meaning for the garment's creator and wearer.

As a "cultural object" that participates in language (in this case, the Romanian language), the IA also serves as a marker of belonging within specific communities. Minca's decision to wear an IA throughout the film itself is an argument, allowing Minca not only to ally herself with the Romanian state, but also to suggest an increased cooperation between the Roma and non-Roma through the fashion they share. In what is always a polarized climate between Roma and non-Roma groups, this symbol joins one of the many gaps between these two communities, and even argues, if we adopt Szeman's notion of the "citizenship gap," that such a gap is lessening because of experiences like the ones shared in the film. Ultimately, this defines the fashion of citizenship and argues that the Roma witches should be accepted because they dress and act like Romanian citizens.

I'm also interested in another argument made through Minca's decision to wear the IA—an ancillary decision in which she welcomes Larsson into her home and lets her borrow an IA to wear during the first herb spell she participates in (fig. 9). This decision suggests that Minca is so comfortable with using the IA as a national symbol[4] that she's willing to welcome a stranger into her home and share this national symbol with an outsider. It would be difficult to argue against such generosity, but I'm interested in how this decision actually advances an argument for the reconciliation of the Roma within the Romanian mainstream. If, for instance, Minca, who shares Roma heritage, is willing to welcome a non-Roma outsider and thus set an example for the mainstream to follow after viewing their

---

4   A national symbol, consequently, which is not thought of as her own.

celebratory representation in the film, what's to say that the mainstream shouldn't also send these same reconciliatory messages to the Roma? In this respect, Minca's decision to share the IA with Larsson speaks volumes for the status of the "citizenship gap," allowing Minca to leverage cultural history that she herself isn't seen as owning while also advancing an argument for increased inclusivity between Roma and non-Roma groups. Minca grants Larsson Roma citizenship in the same way that Minca herself is advocating for the Roma's full inclusion within mainstream Romanian culture. This can be read as another move to authorize the existence of Roma culture in the eyes of a clearly Westernized outsider, which is significant because it places Larsson in a position to use the platform of documentary film to advance arguments about Roma acceptance. The IA, although not a garment associated with witchcraft by any means, authorizes Roma identity, which in turn is placed in more productive light with the understanding that it's so easily shared with a non-Roma outsider like Larsson who carries the weight of representing the entire community to the global world.

Finally, according to Corduneanu and Dragan:

> Wearing [the IA] for a social gathering, be it a religious festival or the traditional dance on Sundays, made it easy for people to know your exact place of birth, social and marital status but also your personality and virtues and they could decide, at a glance, if it was worthy to approach you in any way. Because the eyes of the people from the past could 'scan' your IA and get the message.

Minca's decision to proudly wear the IA and to even share in the IA's symbolism with an outsider reveals an interesting alliance between the country of Romania and the practice of witchcraft. What's the argument here? Simply put, when Minca wears the IA and invokes it as a national symbol, she challenges the place of witchcraft within the Romanian state and argues for the increased acceptance of state-sanctioned witchcraft. Later, I will consider the how the Romanian government sanctions specific forms of witchcraft through the use of taxes, but the seeds of this are planted in this decision, allowing the IA to participate, as Corduneanu and Dragan demonstrate, in the language of nationalism and the language of witchcraft.

These two details, the style of performative speech and the IA, allow the witches to participate in a performance of witchcraft. This performance, as I've suggested, is crucial to the survival of Roma witchcraft culture because it allows them to enter accepted modes of expression and perform an aspect of "civility" that works to build their case for granting citizenship in Romania. This performance authorizes the existence of Roma identity by demonstrating a lineage of actions and essentially advancing another argument that the Roma should be taken seriously. Other scholars have agreed with this point, isolating how sharing speech and narrative are central to the witchcraft tradition, arguing for "the strong connection between witchcraft and narrative tradition": "Witchcraft beliefs were maintained and passed on in traditional forms of narratives, and people turned to certain narrative patterns when reporting about their own experiences—either in the courtroom or when talking to their peers." This is not difficult to believe, given the prevalent role speech plays in the transmission of witchcraft history. In this light, it's easier to understand that what the Minca witches are engaged in during the film is a complex performance of witchcraft that relies on mixing "traditional forms of narratives,"—in Minca's case, the herb spell—with new "narrative patterns"—in Buzea's case, the anecdote she shares about being arrested for practicing witchcraft. Ultimately, the goal of all of these engagements is acceptance, reconciliation, and ultimately, as Szeman points out, a path to citizenship.

More broadly, without the show that is Roma witchcraft, along with its deeply stylized rendition through *Vice News*, the Roma are effectively silenced by a larger, louder mainstream culture that has enough material (in form of stereotype and xenophobic tropes) to silence and figuratively destroy the Roma in their entirety. As such, the self-referentiality these witches use to perform their characters is representative of the Roma's larger cultural signalizing, a demand to be heard, appreciated, and listened to.

Measuring the Effects of Modernity on Witchcraft

In this same light, it would be a mistake not consider modernity's effects on witchcraft, specifically the rendition of witchcraft in the film. By modernity, I simply mean a modernized version of traditional witchcraft—a version that in this case, still relies on traditional images and tropes: tarot cards, broom sticks, herbs and spells, and the cauldron fire. In doing so, I rely on the quoted assertion above, that "Witchcraft beliefs were maintained and passed on in traditional forms of narratives, and people turned to certain narrative patterns." Here, I'm concerned with the specific comments the Minca witches make about the practice of witchcraft, but as I do in the previous section, I maintain that these comments are self-referential, ultimately theatrical, and designed to build Roma acceptance and citizenship.

Asking Minca to reflect on her practice, Larsson inquires, "Are you worried that modern times will change this ancient craft?" Minca responds, "Nu, nu, nu-l va afecta. Dimpotrivă, va face cunoscută în întreaga lume că puterea noastră există. Deci oamenii cred." ("No, no, no, it won't affect it. On the contrary, it'll make it known worldwide that our power exists. So that people believe.") Here, Minca reinstates the place of witchcraft in the contemporary world, arguing from the basis that it's needed now more than ever, and that its impetus is bolstered by the fact that "our power exists." This comment supports the necessity of keeping Roma witches like Minca around and easily accessible to the public. It also hearkens back to Kristen Sollée's assertion that the witch is "having a moment," a moment Minca will capitalize on as a result of this film. (In chapter 3, I will discuss the specific ways that witchcraft cashes in on this "moment," implicating market capitalism to ultimately bridge the occult with the secular.) Nevertheless, Minca's comment arrives in the larger cultural moment we inhabit, a moment that is seeing the proliferation and acceptance of popular witchcraft. This proliferation is impossible to achieve without the transmission of witch narratives through language.

Along with asking the witches to reflect on their profession, Larsson asks a series of compelling questions about the profession's evolution since the witches began practicing. Of Buzea, she asks, "What was witchcraft like when you were a kid?" Buzea responds, "Era mai rar ca oamenii să ne ceară să facem rău cuiva. Cele mai multe vrăji au fost pentru prosperitate, bogăție, căsătorie și bunăstare. Acum, cei mai mulți dintre ei trebuie să trimită răul vrăjmașilor." ("It was rarer that people would ask us to harm someone. Most spells were for prosperity, wealth, marriage and well-being. Now most of them are to send evil to one's enemies.") This comment suggests a turn from witchcraft being used for noble purposes to now being used for harm. I read this turn as emblematic of the capitalistic structure we inhabit, an idea I address in chapter 3, when I consider market capitalism's effects on witchcraft. Of course, it's hard to argue with the profitability of the Minca witches, but this comment alone suggests a transition in the profession that will be important to keep in mind moving forward.

The comment also establishes historical lineage, allowing Minca to argue for her continued existence and acceptance from the basis that she's a Roma woman with a distinct heritage. This argument authorizes her to combat the stereotype that Roma are "too poor to have culture," an idea Ioana Szeman broaches at great length.

Even Larsson isolates this turn from good to evil after listening to a curse Minca shares: "Trimiteți un blestem tuturor vrăjmașilor mei și celor care vorbesc rău despre numele meu, să se transforme în praf, cu excepția familiei, a nepoților și a fiicelor mele." ("Send a curse to all my enemies and those who speak badly of my name, may they turn into dust, apart from my family, nieces, and daughters.") She asks Minca, "Do you ever feel guilty when you do spells like this?" who responds, "Nu mă simt vinovat pentru că asta e treaba mea. Uneori îl întreb pe Dumnezeu pentru iertare. Dar asta face o vrăjitoare: face bine și face rău. Cu diavolul și cu sfântul. În loc să plătească mafia pentru a răni pe cineva, pentru al tăia sau a-l ucide, este mai bine să plătești o vrăjitoare care să-l facă să-și piardă banii și averea." ("I don't feel guilty because this is my job. Sometimes I ask God for forgiveness. But that's what a witch does: she does good and she does bad. With the devil and with the saint. Instead of paying the Mafia to harm someone, to cut him or kill him, it's better to pay a witch to make a curse to make him lose his money and fortune.") In this performance of witchcraft, Minca discloses the fact that the profession has always been in transition, continually forced to tow the line between committing acts of good and evil. Although it appears tongue-in-cheek for an American audience, Minca's comment that rather than "paying the Mafia," people can now contract Roma witches to cast curses, should be read as a deadpan acknowledgement that witchcraft is a convenient albeit pricy alternative to physical violence.

Finally, modernity's effects on Roma witchcraft are felt in how the film comments on Roma/non-Roma relations through Larsson's interactions with her subject. According to one scholar, "Ca o regulă, ghicitoarele nu folosesc ghicitul cu alți țigani. În comunitatea lor, țiganii au alte modalități a preveni viitorul și a vindeca." ("As a rule, fortune tellers do not use fortune telling with other gypsies. In their community, [gypsies] have other methods of predicting the future and vindicating." This is significant for relations between Roma and non-Roma represented in the film, but it also suggests that the profession of Roma witchcraft is positioned in response to some Other, which in this case is the non-Roma mainstream. This unsuspecting reversal, where non-Roma Romanians can be seen as Other, complicates our understanding of Roma/non-Roma relations, arguing that each group authorizes the other through the figure of the witch that both are forced to interact with. This noteworthy reversal flips the power dynamics between Roma and non-Roma and *places the non-Roma in a position of subservience* to the Roma witches, whose access to the occult privileges them for the time being. Thus, the non-Roma come to benefit from and actually depend on the Roma's occult knowledge and labor practices, a group that's continually being pushed out from the mainstream despite being increasingly relied on for its knowledge of the occult.

Another result of global media liberalization is the proliferation of lower-cost, high-impact genres such as the variety show, the talk show—in both its lowbrow and highbrow variations—and more importantly, the now ubiquitous reality genre and its many subtypes. These genres have in common an absence or minimal presence of highly paid talent, low-cost studio or outdoor production, and a tendency toward the raw, bizarre, and sensational.

—Marwan Kraidy, *Hybridity, Or the Cultural Logic of Globalization*

Chapter Three

VICE NEWS AS A MEDIATOR OF AMERICAN CULTURE

Founded in 1994 by Shane Smith and Suroosh Alvi, *Vice* began as a platform catering to the "funny, hip, and off-color," to stories that didn't always conform with the standards of international journalism. In this chapter, I outline the platform's history, placing it in the context of "Casting Curses and Love Spells," the film I introduce in the previous chapter. Then, I present a critique of *Vice News* for what it's become, a mediator of American culture.

'Under-Reported Stories,' Shock Value, and Manufactured Intrigue

From its inception as *Vice Magazine*, the platform was determined to report on the "under-reported," mixing the stories they produced with a heavy drug culture that permeated all levels of their production staff. Founder Shane Smith was tantamount on "producing an entertaining, purposely offensive lad mag at a time when Maxim and others were in vogue," which allowed him to position *Vice* in opposition to the magazine journalism of the time through a new standoffish insistence on reporting the stories others either didn't want to report or knew they shouldn't be reporting. In her authoritative retelling of the platform's history, *Merchants of Truth: The Business of News and the Fight for Facts*, Jill Abramson writes how part of *Vice's* motto has always been the tacit understanding that it "'paid to be perceived as edgy,'" quoting directly from Smith, whose goal became to marry the edginess of the moment they inhabited with their insatiable thirst for involving a new generation of media consumers, millennials. From its beginning, *Vice* targeted this demographic with its response to the fact that "Young people age 18 to 29 were the least likely to watch network news regularly; nearly half said they never watched the news. Almost no one in this age group could even name a network anchor. This was the same buying demographic that advertisers were desperate to reach, and it was *Vice's* sweet spot." By marketing the edgy and by marketing it *online*, Smith tapped into what he envisioned would be a voracious consumer of news media. He wasn't wrong.

As Abramson writes, *Vice* responded to the fact that "young people were turned off by TV news, not because they weren't interested in the world but because of how the news was presented." Clearly, this was a framing issue. To counteract this, the platform focused on employing "visual thinkers," content creators who were willing and able to produce high-quality, visually-appealing infographics, documentaries, and films that could then be marketed on platforms such as *YouTube*. Abramson also points out just how quickly *Vice* began to eclipse traditional media when it came to successfully targeting a younger demographic with its documentaries and films: "The Times and Post hired a few videographers and assigned them to follow print reporters, posting video doppelgangers of their stories. But the print reporters always took the lead and didn't know how to enhance their journalism with the new digital tools." With the competition underway, *Vice* continued to excel, its success largely a result of the shock value they managed to create with early films, including "The Islamic State," one of its most famous films which documented jihadi terror and is alleged to have indirectly supported terrorism. About this film, *The Atlantic* asked, "Is *Vice's* Documentary on ISIS Illegal?" Edginess, once again, won out.

The Atlantic had a similar reaction to *Vice's* covering of sobering relations between North Korea and the US, mediated as it became apparent, by NBA star Dennis Rodman. Producing the edgy headline, "Why Is *Vice* Hiding Its Kim Jong-un Interview?" it's easy to see how *The Atlantic* not only bought into the hype *Vice* actively marketed—a hype initially deployed for a younger demographic, remember—but also promoted it, playing to *Vice's* target demographic by authorizing these types of questions in the first place. By this point, *Vice* has managed to evolve from the platform media moguls like the *New York Times*, *The Washington Post*, and *The Atlantic* avoided to the platform they emulated.

One of the reasons for *Vice's* continued success is its insistence on manufacturing intrigue. In addition to its ability to easily create shock value by going to places where other journalists aren't willing to go, *Vice* capitalizes on manufacturing intrigue in its target demographic by directly identifying and covering stories of Others, of individuals and communities on the periphery of mainstream society. *Vice* is willing to take the risk for any failures (both cultural and fiscal), which sets them ahead of the game in the documentary film world. *Vice* is also able to manufacture intrigue in its audience's minds, arguing that good journalism is synonymous with dangerous experiences, and that the documentary filmmakers it sends out are noble partially for their willingness to interact with communities and situations that more conservative groups would shy away from out of pure fear.

Vice suggests that good journalism is dangerous, that the best stories have some element of physical and psychological risk in them, and that the best films document and then transcend this risk, putting forth a narrative tradition built upon a self-congratulatory ethos.[1] One of the most obvious places this is located is on their website's Submissions page. As of this writing, the Submissions page includes instructions for five different ways that people can submit tips for potential stories and films. Most of these methods are anonymous, with clear disclaimers warning people about this, should they be interested in submitting a story. *Vice* is also careful to include the following disclaimer about being a whistle blower:

> Remember that if you want to be truly anonymous in your correspondence with us, you'll have to use a phone number that's not associated with your real identity. This means buying a SIM card with cash, and without providing an identification number. In most cases, this extreme step will likely not be necessary: Please think about what steps you may need to take depending on what information you'd like to provide, and who you are trying to avoid detection from. For the majority of instances, using Signal [*Vice's* anonymous tip platform] on a personal phone (not a work-owned one) will work great.

Aside from passing on completely obvious information—being a whistle blower has consequences in our media saturated

---

1   It would be interesting to subject Joseph Mitchell's profile of Johnny Nikanov to this claim. Granted, that would also involve a keen discussion of the dynamics of truth, falsehood, and journalistic integrity.

world—this disclaimer's main purpose is to suggest that good journalism involves placing oneself in dangerous situations, in situations that demand anonymity—situations, in other words, that *do* call for one to "avoid detection," to use a very paranoid connection between information and fear. One could argue that this disclaimer is useful for the populations of citizen journalists who submit stories from parts of the world that do not protect press freedom, but it's important to remember that a majority of *Vice's* stories originate in the US, suggested not by citizens, but by staff members. Ultimately, this disclaimer helps *Vice* manufacture intrigue in the journalistic profession, which allows them to argue that good journalism is dangerous and as a result, that journalists who are willing to experience this danger (*Vice* journalists, surprise!) deserve recognition.[2]

Finally, it's important to note that the platform hasn't always been without controversy. In fact, in more ways than one, controversy has been its defining characteristic. Throughout her retelling of *Vice's* history, Abramsom never shies away from stating the obvious: on account of their mainly white male staff, *Vice* has always struggled with allegations of sexual harassment and non-inclusivity, two souring details that are difficult to recover from today. Abramson writes, "[At *Vice News*] the supervisors were almost all male, and sexual liaisons between bosses and young associate producers were common. […] There was a huge problem, too, with sexual harassment, incidents that unspooled after work at bars, often following long drinking sessions." She goes so far as to characterize this culture of sexual

---

2   To be clear, I'm not arguing that journalists who are willing to experience danger in order to write, publish, and share news stories do not deserve recognition. Rather, I'm here concerned with how *Vice* uses this willingness to experience danger as a self-congratulatory reflection on themselves and the news industry at large.

harassment as "endemic," identifying other news outlets—the *Daily Beast*, for instance—that published pieces vehemently attacking *Vice* for its inability to build a workplace culture of safety and acceptance. It is, after all, 2019.[3]

Hybridity and Uses-And-Gratifications

According to Jill Abramson, *Vice* is always "looking for authenticity, [hoping] to attract a generation that could smell any hint of fakeness." This a fine mission statement that clearly identifies a target demographic, but what happens next? How is it that *Vice* is able to translate this energy into appealing content? In this section, I grapple with these two questions while also considering how *Vice* serves as a mediator of American culture. As always, the Roma witches are never far away, appearing in my discussion of how *Vice* frames them for a predominantly American audience. Although this analysis extends to many other films *Vice* produces, I will limit myself to the Roma witches for the sake of clarity, but the critique presented in this

---

3　　At the end of her discussion of *Vice*, Abramson situates the platform within the Trump Era, which has influenced journalism as much as any other avenue of professional American life. She writes: "Times had changed. In the pre-Weinstein and pre-fake-news era, *Vice* might have gone unpunished for its shenanigans, from workplace harassment to shoddy standards. But in the Trump era, the news media were under more scrutiny. As the conduit for report after report of misconduct and alleged corruption, the news media had to adhere to higher standards. Smith had bragged that *Vice* would replace both CNN and Time magazine in the pantheon of respected news organizations." Time will only tell how far this will extend into the future and to what extent *Vice's* reputation in the journalistic world will continue to help or hurt the films it produces.

section can also apply to other films produced by the platform. By considering *Vice* a *mediator* of American culture, I assume:

1. *Vice* has access to subjects traditionally outside most American's interests and immediate contact.

2. *Vice* presents a reading of their subjects inside the film of the Roma witches. This reading, in turn, is colored by a set of predominantly Americanized expectations that allow them to cater to an American target demographic.

3. How *Vice* chooses to present this reading to their audience interacts with popularly-accepted beliefs about traditional witchcraft, ultimately marrying these beliefs with the new ones *Vice* extracts from the Roma community.

For this discussion, I rely on the notion of hybridity, borrowing from the work of Henrik Bødker, one of the first academics to publish about *Vice News*. Bødker best defines hybridity as the "bringing together of seemingly contradictory elements," using the term to ask, "whether *Vice News* is a promising rethinking of journalism or a sign of its debasement." Bødker weaves an analysis of *Vice's* coverage of the events in Ferguson, Missouri (2014) throughout his discussion of hybridity and articulates an argument for the increased relevance of studying platforms like *Vice*. I use Bødker's piece to reinstate the importance of thinking about how *Vice* frames certain events, albeit using the platform to draw a different conclusion about a very different community. From this perspective, I argue that Bødker's decision to couch *Vice's* success in its ability to navigate hybridity on page and screen is productive and apply this same dynamic to my discussion of the Roma witches.

"Casting Curses and Love Spells with the Most Powerful Witches in Romania" relies on hybridity in the form of the following tensions: that between good and evil, between traditional and contemporary witchcraft, and between Americanized reporting and Romanian subjects. *Vice* frames these tensions productively, forcing them to interact on the world stage it provides by creating its film. In this respect, *Vice* serves as a mediator of American culture. It interprets, frames, and publishes a rendition of the Roma witches' existence by relying on the aforementioned hybrid elements. These elements, in turn, become interesting and highly marketable to *Vice's* target demographic. Hybridity, I maintain, is highly profitable for a platform like *Vice*, bent as it is on including multiple perspectives and foreign cultures. Diversity is thus expensive—and highly profitable.

This discussion also subscribes to what Marwan Kraidy terms the "uses-and-gratifications" theory of media consumption. For Kraidy, audience members are 1. "...motivated to make conscious choices about which media to use," and 2. "know how to use them in order to obtain gratification." Drawing on extensive psychological research to reach this point, Kraidy articulates exactly what the typical *Vice* audience member experiences—a pre-selection of films that are viewed "in order to obtain gratification." As I've argued, one of the ways that *Vice* does this is by engaging the hybrid elements of multiple cultures.

As Kraidy points out:

> The deregulation of media and telecommunications has entailed the withdrawal of the state as an active manager of national broadcasting, and the concomitant rise in importance of the multinational corporations that now control much of world media activities.

This is especially important to consider given just how political a position the Roma occupy in Romania. Their representation on *Vice*, then, serves as an outlet to share their culture with a mainstream audience, bolstered by the understanding that this audience has already bought into *Vice's* journalistic mission. Even Kraidy picks up on this: "These developments explain why television programs are increasingly hybrid, embedded with signs and symbols with transregional appeal, and executed in line with the imperative of market expansion." For the Roma, who have been previously victimized by state-run propaganda missions, *Vice* serves as an inclusive, heterogenous platform willing and able to share their story with the mainstream. But it would be a mistake to stop here, arguing only that *Vice creates* exposure for an under-reported group. By having access to a community that most audiences will never have access to and by using its position of power to represent this audience to a global world that's clearly interested in learning from what *Vice* has to offer, the platform authorizes the Roma's place within Romanian culture. By representing the Minca witches—not an unbiased representation by any means—*Vice* uses documentary film to authorize the existence of Roma women as a distinct sub-culture operating in mainstream Romania, and thus confirms what has always been a suspicious question when it comes to women and witches: Should we take them seriously? In the spirit of documentary film, the answer always seems to be *yes*, but this is an unparalleled response given the entrenched history of exclusion from all avenues of cultural representation that the Roma have experienced. Ultimately, through the (biased) exposure it provides, *Vice* authorizes this community's existence in an American audience's eyes, serving as a biased mediator that's willing to advance the argument that these Roma women deserve to be positively represented and accepted in their daily lives.

It is in this spirit that the Roma are able to produce national mythology. As Lucian Boia suggests, for the non-Roma, national mythology involves invoking figures such as Vlad Tepes, King Carol I, and King Mihai I, which serve as cultural capital implying a clearly Romanian lineage. These are mythological figures who represent a concrete, identifiable history that can serve to include and exclude communities who identify or do not identify, who honor or do not honor these figures. This is a strategic invocation of history. The Roma, however, do not have access to this national mythology, and instead use witchcraft as a substitute for these foundational myths. In this light, then, *Vice News* is seen as the stage where these new foundational myths are exercised and shared with the public.

Why, then, doesn't this translate well to the Romanian public? Why, for instance, would some Romanian citizens shy away from this type of film? I distinctly remember watching this film with a Romanian friend living in the United States. Aside from laughing at some of the obvious cultural faux pas Larsson commits, my friend couldn't help but share, at the end, that all the film accomplishes is to depict an "unpleasant" aspect of Romanian society for the global public. When pressed to define just what he meant by "unpleasant," he confirmed my suspicion—the Roma.

Part of this framing issue involves understanding that of the little coverage Romania receives internationally (here I partially excuse Kraidy who isn't necessarily concerned with one country in particular), most of it isn't congratulatory. The headlines about Romania in popular American publications included in chapter one attest to this. Even "uses-and-gratifications" theory argues for the dissemination of media that will *gratify* rather than upset. But this isn't to excuse my friend's dislike for the Roma or the implicit argument he was making that part of his problem is that what many Americans know about Romania revolves around the Roma. Rather, this requires us to understand that what is *not* shown makes as strong an argument as what *is* shown. I'm not excusing the fact that my friend referred to the Roma as an unpleasant aspect of Romanian culture; rather, I point out that this statement also involved an unstated argument for increasing global exposure of issues and events happening in Romania.[4] Through its decision to cover this story, *Vice* is not only tasked with upholding the tenets of international journalism (a feat they have certainly not lived up to in their storied past) but also presenting film honestly, and with the clear goal of entertainment in mind.

Measuring the Effects of Vice as a Mediator of American Culture

I began this book by identifying the historical distance that separates Joseph Mitchell's profile of Johnny Nikanov (1942) from *Vice News'* filmography (2016), but have said little about

---

4   A few years ago, I remember watching an episode of Anthony Bourdain's *No Reservations* that took place in Romania with a few first-generation Romanian friends. Bourdain and his friend Zamir find themselves in Romania with the goal of celebrating Zamir's birthday in Romanian pomp and circumstance. Picking up on the fact that Zamir is not actually Romanian, and thus Bourdain couldn't be bothered even to consult with a native, my friends were also disturbed by the fact that a majority of the trip was spent in a binging, alcoholic coma. Of course, I hyperbolize, but I attest that these comments were one of the first that set me on my research goal to evaluate the way specific aspects of Romanian culture are framed in American media.

this concrete *history*. Having defined both the Roma witch as my subject and *Vice News* as my medium, it's now helpful to briefly outline the American history separating Mitchell from *Vice News*. Doing so allows us to measure the effects of this *American* representation in the absence of a quantitative study on media representation, a task that is beyond this project's scope, which is solely concerned with literary representation.

In the seventy-year space that separates Mitchell from *Vice News*, it would be impossible to ignore the power and prevalence of another witchy cultural moment that took place: the rise in power, acceptance, and legitimation of Wicca. In her book, *Witches of America*, Alex Mar situates Wicca within the increasingly prevalent belief of the 1950s that the "divine can be found within us and all around us, and that we can communicate regularly with the dead and the gods without a priestly go-between." Mar outlines Wicca's origins in Britain at the hands of Gerald Gardner and traces its history in the US through one of Gardner's initiates, who went on to found the "first known Wiccan coven in America," in New York State. Given its insistence on locating the divine within the individual practitioner, it's easy to see why Wicca became so popular in the United States, a country whose national mythology is founded on the assertion of personal over institutional power, on individuality over collectivity.

By the 1960s, some 20 years after Mitchell's sensationalist profile of Johnny Nikanov, "...word about Wicca had spread, and many were eager to be initiated, without nearly enough covens to train them." Mar outlines how those who turned to Wicca claimed they had "finally found the belief system to give shape and meaning to their lives" and worked to define this new occult practice through "improvised spins on the tradition." Mar's retelling of Wiccan history is compelling for a host of reasons, notwithstanding how it capitalizes on American individualism during the turbulent 60s, but it also marks a moment—arguably one of the first—in American history where practicing witchcraft authorizes the existence of an Other, of those whose fringe beliefs could now be named and married with a slowly growing social practice. Eventually, the practice became so prevalent that it was acceptable for a person to "self-initiate" into Wicca, to call and cast themselves as a member of this occult practice and thus, to adopt a previously-denied identity as a move of empowerment.[5] I'm not interested in suggesting similarities and differences between Wicca and Roma witchcraft; admittedly, there are many. Rather, I'm concerned with how American culture casts both of these practices. I aim to position Wicca as a brief case study in what *can* happen to Roma witchcraft based on what *did* happen to Wicca as its increasing prevalence is still felt today. In *Vice News'* hands, Roma witchcraft will have to contend with these same dynamics as it continues to define a space in American consciousness, just as Mitchell's Nikanov did in 1942.

First Nikanov, then Wicca, then the Roma witches. But if we're going to use Wicca as a case study to assess the effects of witchcraft beliefs on the American public, we'd miss an entire side of the argument, the legal side, which itself authorizes the practice of witchcraft in American culture. One of the most compelling moments for this argument occurred in 1986, when the US Court of Appeals for the Fourth Circuit, "declar[ed] the Church of Wicca to be a religion." The case involved Herbert Dettmer, who in 1982, began studying witchcraft through "a correspondence course provided by the Church of Wicca."

---

5   This is the same move of empowerment that contemporary witchcraft encourages.

Dettmer, who was incarcerated at the time, requested that the prison allow him to purchase a set of products he claimed were essential for properly practicing Wicca. These products included sulfur, a quartz clock with an alarm, candles, incense, and a white robe. The prison warden refused, citing that the items Dettmer requested were considered "contraband." Dettmer sued, alleging that the prison denied his First Amendment right to practice religion, and claiming that rather than contraband, the items he requested to purchase—with his own money—were articles of faith required to properly practice Wicca. The case is significant in American law for a host of reasons, but I cite it to establish the legal interaction Dettmer must go through in order to authorize his practice of the occult. Eventually, the Circuit Court ruled that "We affirm the district court's judgment that the doctrine proclaimed by the Church of Wicca is a religion entitling Dettmer to the protection that the first amendment affords prisoners." This reveals how the law (usually thought secular) is involved in a complex negotiation between the state and the occult; this is not a groundbreaking conclusion, but it indicates that in twentieth-century America, these negotiations were becoming increasingly prevalent and important to how the American public viewed the practice of the occult.[6] Wicca's rise in America serves as a case study in what could happen to the Roma witches represented by *Vice News*, witches who are clearly different from Joseph Mitchell's profile, yet share Wicca's belief that the occult is a move of empowerment, regardless of the legislation enacted to challenge it.

Finally, I wish to suggest how Wicca represents a transitional moment, a historical bridge between Joseph Mitchell's

---

6   Consequently, this is now the case in contemporary Romania, which, as Alexandra Cotofană argues, is involved in "governing with magic."

representation of Roma culture and *Vice News'*. A series of contrasts between Mitchell and *Vice News* will be helpful to point out. First, Mitchell's profile of Nikanov, as published in *The New Yorker*, can be considered high-brow literature, given both the platform publishing it and the literary style this profile is written in. This strikes a contrast with *Vice's* representation of the Roma witches, which is clearly intended for a younger, millennial audience. Second, Mitchell's profile relies on cultural stereotype to create an uncongratulatory representation of his Roma subject. On the other hand, *Vice's* representation of the Roma witches interacts with cultural stereotypes differently, giving the witches an opportunity to profit (culturally, fiscally) as a result of their stereotyped representation in the film. The witches profit from misrepresentation, an idea I address in chapter 5.

Originating in England, Wicca shares its expatriate status of migration to the United States with Roma culture (both in Mitchell and *Vice News*), which begins in neither Romania nor the United States, but finds its way to these two countries to engage with the question of authority. Wicca, thus, serves as a transitional space to bridge Mitchell with *Vice News* because it uses the occult as a move of empowerment that is distinctly American. Through its interaction with a moment in American history that accepts religious occultism (namely the 40s, 50s, and 60s), Wicca lays the groundwork for a platform like *Vice News* to thrive, a platform that capitalizes on representing and celebrating the Occult and the Other while simultaneously celebrating the spirit of dangerous American journalism. In how it composes its filmography, *Vice* mediates the concerns its audience will experience—mediating, in other words, how Americans will see and understand Roma witchcraft.

It is impossible therefore to associate capitalism with any form of liberation or attribute the longevity of the system to its capacity to satisfy human needs.

—Silvia Federici, *Caliban and the Witch: Women, The Body and Primitive Accumulation*

I'm curious to find out what people pay her for her services.

—Milène Larsson, "Casting Curses and Love Spells with the Most Powerful Witches in Romania"

Chapter Four

UNDERSTANDING THE ROMA WITCHES' LABOR PRACTICES

I'm tempted to ask Larsson's question, too. But in a slightly different light, positioning it alongside Silvia Federici's critical scholarship. In her book *Caliban and the Witch: Women, The Body and Primitive Accumulation*, Federici grapples with the dynamic interplay between market capitalism and the destruction of the female body. Although a text specifically about witchcraft in the early modern period, Federici's analysis is useful to apply to Roma witchcraft as it extends into the twenty-first century because it helps deconstruct the critical underpinning of profit that leads Minca to continue her "family witch business" (WB) in the first place. Along with the self-referential quality of Minca's witchcraft, I propose that her WB is a discrete, capital-producing entity that comes under the regulation of legislation and taxation. Minca's profit motive may be impossible to overcome for the informed observer like Larsson, who asks her question in good, curious faith, but it's also led government officials to speculate on the WB's economic value in particular and the Roma Witchcraft Economy (WE) in general as it extends across the Roma community. In this chapter, I argue that market capitalism and Roma witchcraft are intimately connected and consequently produce a distinct, ahistorical anxiety about the Roma's status in present-day Europe. This anxiety is ahistorical because, although it follows a larger tradition of mass hysteria against witches throughout the early modern period and beyond, it is here positioned through strategic organization, legislation, and ultimately taxation. The narrative, in other words, has shifted from an early modern world obsessed with the violent legislation of witchcraft, to a contemporary world fascinated with the profit motive (however meek) resulting from the Roma witches, and the subsequent legislation that can help reign in and redirect that profit toward the state, whose unique anxiety about witchcraft is subsumed (and overcome) by the profits of taxation. Today, the Romanian state expresses a bidimensional message about the future of Roma witchcraft: on one hand, it purports a *façade* of anxiety about the totemism, voodoo, herbalism, fortunetelling, and spell-casting of the WB to the *public*; on the other, it uses this same fabricated façade to strike economic fear into the already destitute Roma community, who are repeatedly offered the cultural messages of redemption and reconciliation as the ultimate prizes if they reject their witchcraft and return to the legislated market capitalism the state argues they belong in.[1]

Male Anxiety and the Tax on Witches

It's useful to begin by addressing the obsessive profit motive that *Vice* draws out from the WB represented in its film. Mihaela Minca is, first and foremost, a capital-producing entity.

---

1   By "public," I refer to media channels such as the interview Larsson conducts with Alin Popoviciu.

As a result, her filmic representation argues that she's successful given market capitalism's confines; she produces enough capital (we're led to believe) to sustain her family. Even Larsson herself, who is deeply entrenched in these concerns, speculates, "I'm curious to find out what people pay her for her services." After all, according to the billboard hanging outside her home, Minca is, "Romania's Most Powerful Witch" who manages to take phone calls and give consultations while cooking and cleaning. The film claims that on average, Minca has 3 – 4 clients per day. The question of female celebrity complicates this since Minca is known all over Romania, and in her eyes, all over the world, too. (She could, of course, be overselling herself.)

It's easy to see how this could become a legislative problem should hundreds of other witches operate alongside Minca, reaping profits across the EU without paying taxes. Contributing to this anxiety, Larsson reminds, "Romania's witch economy is worth at least a million Euros a year and they are all doing it tax free!" a figure that's difficult to corroborate, but a figure that nonetheless reappears throughout the film, thus sanctioning the statistic through the exposure it receives from *Vice*. Apart from the profit Minca makes, which we're left to speculate on, the film argues that she's also successful because she has managed to instill an adequate fear in the minds of legislators, who proposed a tax against Roma witches to curb the alleged profits they make. This tax, represented in the *New York Times*' article "A Tax on Witches? A Pox on the President," argues that:

> In the past, the less mainstream professions of witch, astrologer and fortuneteller were not listed in the Romanian labor code, and people who worked in those jobs used their lack of registration to evade paying income tax. Under a new law, they will pay 16 percent income tax and make contributions to health and pension programs, like other self-employed people.

As Caroline Humphrey posits, the regulation of witchcraft through taxation is possible because "modernity and witchcraft are compatible systems." The law thus represents a novel casting of an older trend: the making known, making understood, and making powerful of the witchcraft tradition to the greater Romanian culture, which has repeatedly denigrated the Roma's operation in any realm of the sociocultural sphere—until the possibility of profit by taxation presents itself. In this section, I suggest that regulating witchcraft involves regulating Roma women's actions—keeping close tabs and fiscal policy on the daily lives of strong women who are leaders in their communities. The government, in turn, is tasked with responding through legislation, something they're already comfortable doing when it comes to regulating Roma life.

To the mainstream, Minca's WB demonstrates its success by creating capital; the reactionary legislation proposed by the Romanian parliament, however, represents a distinct, illogical anxiety about creating Roma capital that only serves to reinstate its anxiety about the existence of this nomadic group of people. In Minca's eyes, the WB has managed to subvert mainstream political allegiances by creating anxiety over regulating Romanian capital. In a country already plagued by corruption, this anxiety must be regulated at all costs, which is best represented through the proposed legislation. Alluding to the law, Alin Popoviciu, MP of the Democratic Liberal Party, encapsulates the fear that led legislators to forfeit the law, "Some of my colleagues had encounters with witches. They preferred not to pass this law, believing something might happen to them." This statement clarifies that even mainstream Romania is not comfortable with the blurred distinctions among witchcraft, magic, and capital. This discomfort, in turn, is tellingly manifested through fiscal legislation. The bridge between anxiety and legislation is best summarized in this comment, taken in the first-hand style *Vice* has become famous for, with Larsson asking the questions and Popoviciu responding deadpan.

In *Governing with Magic: Politics and Labors of the Occult in Romania*, Alexandra Cotofană suggests a link between this same anxiety and the subsequent legislation produced by the Romanian state, situating the anxiety in the ways supposedly secular societies employ the occult:

> The occult is not only a socioeconomic and political tool for the poor, uneducated, rural, and often feminine social actors. Nor is it just a tool of the colonized, and of those marginalized by vocabularies of Third Worlds. The occult is also employed by wealthy, educated, urban, male elites, who govern affluent countries.

Popoviciu qualifies for Cotofană's definition of "wealthy, educated, urban, male [elite]" in so far as he's willing to level a tax on the Roma witches for practicing an aspect of their culture. (As of this writing, the only political representation Roma citizens have in their country's government is the *one* party seat they hold in the Romanian Chamber of Deputies.)[2]

Cotofană goes on to identify how:

> Magic is arguably one of the most contested topics in social research and in everyday life. There is a particular level of pressure on individuals holding political and administrative functions to avoid belief and practice in magic, which has harsh consequences in a period of secularized development, such as communism or adjusting to a politico-economic supra-national project, such as the EU.

But this comment places Popoviciu's comment in new light. If, as Cotofană argues, "There is a particular level of pressure" in

---

2   This seat is held by Nicolae Paun.

political office to "avoid belief and practice in magic," why are Popoviciu and his colleagues still engaged in these questions? Why, in other words, is Popoviciu unafraid to admit the tension between witchcraft and legislation that's arrived right on his desk?

Answering this involves understanding that Popoviciu is proposing legislation that would primarily affect the Roma community, a community that has repeatedly been spoken for rather than spoken with. It's easier for legislators like Popoviciu to level these sorts of claims with the understanding that their proposals will directly affect a community that's still struggling to integrate into mainstream society, a community, after all, that should be *thankful*. This, along with the fact that the Roma hold one seat in their country's representative Parliament, supports the notion that legislation can be passed on the Roma's behalf without consulting public opinion. But his resistance also reveals our cultural moment: tasked with grappling with their anxiety, "these wealthy, educated, urban, male elites" turn to controlling and legislating other people's actions, and more directly, their bodies. Thus, one way to read this legislation is as a deliberate attempt to reconcile male anxiety about strong women in society by creating laws and tax codes. This is disempowering at best and negligent at worst. Later, Silvia Federici will have more to say about this when I consider the role capitalism plays in this discussion.

One way to reconcile this male anxiety, or at the very least to make it better known to the voting public, Cotofană acknowledges, is by continuing to legitimate the profession of witchcraft in the eyes of the law: "On January 1st, 2011, the national tax codes were updated to promote adding witchcraft to the list of jobs in the national labor code." Again, this can be read in three different ways, as an acknowledgement that legislators like Popoviciu are actively interacting with the occult through-out what should legally be a secular profession. It can also be read as an active welcoming effort of Roma women into the capitalist market, though I admit that this seems too hopeful a reading given the destitute poverty many Roma experience. Finally, and most convincingly, it can be read as sharply undercutting the rights and privileges afforded to contemporary women, specifically Roma, in Romania. Once again, Roma women are being spoken for rather than with, consulted only after the fact that laws have been proposed and livelihoods affected. This narrative is certainly not new, especially given the historical precedence Viorel Achim identifies when it comes to the fact that Roma history is often written by non-Roma communities.

Although it's difficult to reconcile this male anxiety entirely, Cotofană provides another productive way to think about it in terms of the Roma Witchcraft Economy which has slowly started growing in Romania:

> Even though Romanian politicians openly oppose vrăjitorie [(witch-craft)], and define the practice as backwards and superstitious, this view does not seem to be supported by the numerous clients that the vrăjitoare have. In fact, the witches enjoyed increasing revenue even during the 2008 economic crisis, according to my interviews with both male and female vrăjitori.

Roma witches, thus, are distinct capital producing entities operating inside a state that's slowly becoming more comfortable with the blurring distinctions between the occult and the secular. It may be too early to propose the future of the Roma Witchcraft Economy, a task I undertake in the following chapter, but the foundations for such an economy are already in place. Even Cotofană, who is careful to make this bridge, goes so far as to suggest that: "We thus come to understand that witchcraft and the modern state function similarly, in part because they are both occult economies." This statement also serves as encouragement for clients who are willing to engage in consultations with Roma witches, such as the woman who visits Minca to receive counseling on her nightmares. When pressed by Larsson to reveal whether or not the woman is paying more by seeing Minca rather than visiting a psychologist, the woman admits that Minca is "A bit more expensive" (fig. 14). She also makes the rhetorical leap required to put the healing services Minca provides on par with those of a psychologist: "the witch is [comparable] to the doctor." These sentiments reveal not only the creating but also the professionalizing of witchcraft in Romania's post-modern economy. The occult has fused with both the legislative and the professional. And it's starting to make money.

It seems impossible, then, for the government to recognize the status of Roma witches without also being forced to tax the profits they make. This reasoning is the result of a distinct anxiety about the creation and proliferation of magic in present-day Romania, which is ultimately encapsulated in the *Times'* coverage of the story referenced earlier in this chapter, "A Tax on Witches? A Pox on the President." A histrionic tone pervades the article while the general, genuine anxiety Romanians actually feel is masked by a humorous headline and an adequate amount of exoticism heaped on the witches. The article repeatedly downgrades the status of Roma witches by positioning them through an ironical tone meant to poke fun at their fight for existence. Phrases like "Everyone curses the taxman," "President Traian Basescu and his aides have been known to wear purple on certain days, supposedly to ward off evil," "…Nicolae Ceaușescu and his wife, Elena, had their own personal witch," and "particularly effective concoction of cat excrement and a dead dog" populate the article. While I don't dispute its factual veracity, it would be difficult to argue that the *Times* itself isn't undercutting these witches' status by positioning them through dubious phraseology, providing further support for the mainstream to use against the Roma. In isolation, this example represents the status of present-day Romania as a country where the tourist is permitted—even encouraged—to exercise their cultural insensitivities, as directed by the *Times'* well-known coverage.

Liberation and the Production of Capital

Today's Roma witches are making money. And if we believe the statistic cited earlier, that "Romania's witch economy is worth at least a million Euros a year and they are all doing it tax free!" they're making serious money. Although I've positioned the potential legislation of the witchcraft profession as a distinct, illogical male anxiety, in what follows, I consider the implications on its female practitioners. Specifically, I grapple with the question of whether or not creating capital is distinctly liberating for a community that's continually been disenfranchised and prevented entry into the mainstream economy.

Consider, for instance, the response Minca gives when asked if she's worried that her clients will renege on their payments: "Chiar dacă clientul nu mă poate plăti în avans, am încredere că vor, pentru că în același mod îmi pot folosi puterile pentru a face bine, este, de asemenea, în puterea mea de a face rău. Nimeni nu vrea să-și asume riscul de a nu mă plăti" ("Even if the client can't pay me in advance I trust they will, because in the same way I can use my powers to do good, it's also within my powers to harm. Nobody wants to take the risk of not paying me.") The assumption here is that while she can use her occult knowledge for good, she can also use it for evil. Through a feminist lens, this comment acknowledges the agency Minca has to determine this on a case-by-case basis. Even further, however, it also suggests that Minca's witch identity is what grants her this move of empowerment, returning us to Kristen Sollée's argument that the witch today is an increasingly productive feminist symbol used by many women for many different purposes—among which, of course, can be evil. In this respect, the witch identity authorizes Minca to participate as an empowered woman, helping her transcend the fact that Roma women are continually demonized and not taken seriously.

Another way to read this as a move of empowerment is to acknowledge how female Roma witches use popular stereotypes to their advantage. In fact, the Minca witches profit (culturally and fiscally) from their *mis*representation, challenging the assertion that Roma women must depend on their husbands to sustain their household both culturally and financially. In this respect, the witches use their stereotyped representation to their advantage, allowing them to strike fear into Romanian legislature and the surrounding hegemonic mainstream that increasingly seeks to push them out. Arguing from the precedence of comments like Popoviciu's, the witches understand when and how to use their stereotyped representation to their advantage, which allows them to partially transcend the disempowered status they're placed in as a result of the fiscal regulation they encounter. Now, they can use the history and mythology that has previously been used against them.

Economically, it may be tempting to read the creation of capital by Minca's WB as a form of liberation from the superstructure of the stratified Romanian economy—a liberation, in turn, that would be utile for the oppressed Roma. According to Federici, however, "It is impossible…to associate capitalism with any form of liberation or attribute the longevity of the system to its capacity to satisfy human needs." The WB may create enough capital to "satisfy human needs," (the Romanian parliament certainly argues that it does, though the picture of rural destitution represented in the film suggests otherwise), but Federici reminds us that an increased dependence on creating capital actually leads to more difficulties, which for the Roma witches, include the need to pay taxes. "One million euros" may be a lot of revenue for one witch in particular, but across the Roma Witch Economy, it's precious little given the demands of living in a contemporary globalized Europe.

As Federici suggests in *Witches, Witch-Hunting, and Women*, an update on her previous scholarship in *Caliban and the Witch*, capitalism has always been concerned with subjugating women's bodies, physically and figuratively. Writing about the history of European capitalism, Federici begins, "female sexuality was both seen as a social threat and, if properly channeled, a powerful economic force." This helps us understand the distinct, male anxiety politicians like Popoviciu are grappling with when they propose and then resist the temptations of taxing female Roma workers. These women's lives are literally in their hands. What's more, Federici insists that "In capitalism, sex can exist but only as a productive force at the service of procreation and the regeneration of the waged/male worker and as a means of social appeasement and compensation for the misery of everyday existence." It's evident from these two quoted passages that Federici is unwilling to see the creation of female labor and profit as anything but oppressive. This is a useful paradigm to apply to the Roma witches because, as I will discuss later in this book, they are repeatedly sent messages of reconciliation and redemption urging them to become productive workers in the

European labor force. When they do, however, they're often hit with regulations and taxes that serve as strategic barriers to entry, never mind the fiscal uncertainty they withstand as a result of politicians like Popoviciu who seem to toy with their futures as if they were another piece of legislation to be written, signed, and passed. However, I will maintain that this is an incomplete reading of the situation since it neglects to identify how the witch identity authorizes the Roma women's entrance into the European economy.

Magic, Witchcraft, and Capitalism

Until now, I've suggested that the witch tax proposed by Romanian legislators is a result of a distinct, male anxiety to regulate women's bodies. Specifically, this regulation involves Roma women, who turn to professions like witchcraft in order to simultaneously honor their heritage and also earn enough money to sustain their livelihoods. In the space that remains, I consider the tension between magic, witchcraft, and capitalism, placing it once again in conversation with Silvia Federici's scholarship.

The tension between magic, witchcraft, and capitalism is not unfounded in witchcraft scholarship. According to Federici:

> Magic, moreover, rested upon a qualitative conception of space and time that precluded a regularization of the labor process. How could the new entrepreneurs impose regular work patterns on a proletariat anchored in the belief that there are lucky and unlucky days, that is, days on which one can travel and others on which one should not move from home, days on which to marry and others on which every enterprise should be cautiously avoided?

Predicating her larger discussion on magic and capitalism within the identification that magic disrupts the control required to make capitalism operate successfully, Federici motions, but does not directly address, that magic is inefficient for capitalism. Efficiency, capitalism's ultimate obsession, cannot by definition be maximized in the presence of magic; it can, however, be utilized toward the aims of the body tasked with regulating the production of capital, the central government, and in Minca's case, the legislature. Often seen as inefficient and demonstrably corrupt, the Romanian government seems best fit to address—with efficiency—the future of Roma witchcraft and how it will directly impact the livelihood of Roma communities. But if Popoviciu's blunder, along with his male colleagues' anxieties about the legitimation of witchcraft in the eyes of the law, is any measure of what the future holds, much will remain the same.

In Minca's case, this conclusion is parodied by the creation of the WB and its assertion of credo as a highly-organized, highly-sustained, and profitable capital producing entity: Minca, a self-proclaimed witch in a post-modern economy, holds consultations with clients while she cooks, sloganizes her own house and permits it to be featured in the *Vice* film, receives a majority of her payments through non-taxable outlets including Western Union and MoneyGram, and, like any skilled freelancer, is hesitant to reveal her actual rate. These details strike a comedic contrast with the superstructure Federici identifies because they represent an ultimate undercutting of the same standards being used to regulate Minca and the Roma witches based on the profits they do make. In what Kristen Sollée would describe as a feminist reinstatement of purpose, they also serve as the ultimate denouncement to wealthy male politicians like Popoviciu who have continued toying with the livelihoods of a Roma community they seem deeply unwilling to understand, learn from, and sympathize with.

At the same time, Minca is unwilling to accept that the profit she makes should be used to gauge her success. Her hesitation to share how much a typical consultation costs also indicates this. This hesitation instills the anxiety required in mainstream Romanian culture to propose and craft legislation such as the witch tax. To bodies like the Romanian government and the *Times*, however, this legislation is presented as their single offer of redemption and reconciliation toward the Roma community, arguing from the basis that participation in a legal, government-mediated European economy is the first step to ensuring a smooth assimilation into the *remainder* of that culture. Cleverly, the existence of such legislation can further be used against the witches if and when they refuse to pay the tax and are then reminded that they themselves, as Roma, have no place in mainstream culture because they do not heed the same hegemonic practices afforded to the mainstream. To Federici, "Eradicating these [magical] practices was a necessary condition for the capitalist rationalization of work, since magic appeared as an illicit form of power and an instrument *to obtain what one wanted without work*, that is, a refusal of work in action." In Romania, magic no longer appears as "an illicit form of power" for two reasons. The first is that the mainstream acknowledges that regardless of whether it deems magic an "illicit form of power," the legal means to enact physical torture on its practitioners is no longer sanctioned under the auspices of governing bodies like the European Union. The second is that Romania today recognizes that the ultimate division between *licit* and *illicit* forms of magic is the profit motive—this motive is what shifts Romania from banning magic to instead legislating it because this creates profit. As Cotofană suggests, this legislation, "would make witches vulnerable to litigation… [and] allow an unsatisfied customer to file a court case against the practitioner of magic," thus bringing the Roma's seemingly nomadic practices into the regulated modernity championed by the EU.

Roma witches will continue taking advantage of politicians like Alin Popoviciu, who occupy a space between completely rejecting witchcraft on the basis that it's ineffective and completely accepting that it can and should be taxed in order to satisfy the larger capitalist superstructure. Although it would be tempting to discredit the possibility of creating a Roma Witchcraft Economy, with all the underpinnings of a traditional post-Communist economy, this is already happening in countries that demonstrate distinct cultural anxieties about the Roma through xenophobia; these anxieties, in turn, are driving legislative policy. The next chapter of this book explores how the fusion of cultural and economic xenophobia has created a state where it's possible—even encouraged—to suggest and then follow through on the legislation required to tax Roma witches. This legislation is problematic because it simultaneously honors the existence of the Roma as practitioners of a genuine, syncretic culture while effectively barring them from the reconciliation, redemption, and success narratives they are fed (and encouraged to act on) by the mainstream.

The Jewish female magician or the Gypsy-witch represent, for the mentality of the peoples that lived in close interdependence with those ethnic groups, great constants of the imaginary, clichés in which historical realities and fantasies, visceral fears and contempt for all that is 'different' and 'alien' melt together.

—Ioan Pop-Curseu, "The Gypsy-Witch: Socio-Cultural Representations, Fascination and Fears"

Chapter Five

Proving Existence Through Tax

Until now, I've considered the distinct economic implications of Roma Witchcraft, going so far as to propose the potential existence of a Roma Witchcraft Economy (WE) as a micro-economy that has tested and will continue to test the strengths of the macroeconomy of post-Communist Romania. I've presented this line of reasoning through the Marxist lens of Silvia Federici. In this chapter, I outline how this economy's under-pinnings—if it is to exist—are largely rooted in the xenophobic context the Roma inhabit in today's Romania, and more largely, in today's Europe. The capitalist anxiety that encourages leaders like Alin Popoviciu to propose the witch tax is driven by the profit motive, and by the xenophobic presentation and stereo-typing of Roma as Other. This presentation excludes the Roma from genuine participation in the Romanian economy while si-multaneously faulting them for refusing to "work hard enough" to ensure their fiscal survival. This discourse of rugged individualism isn't new. In the Roma's case, it's further complicated by the fact that they are presented as Others twice over: the first barring them from practical participation in the mainstream Romanian culture, and by extension economy, and the second by barring them from themselves—inhibiting them from genuinely practicing a self-created identity in lieu of being forced to defend their fiscal and cultural survival inside a xenophobic context that would implicitly prefer to tax them to death. The Roma are double otherized—from Romania and from themselves, in a complex interplay that simultaneously acknowledges its hegemonic existence (Popoviciu's genuine fear of witchcraft) and projects beyond it (in popular, celebratory representations such as those produced by *Vice News*).

The figure of the Roma witch, to use Ioan Pop-Curseu's words, represents a "great [constraint] of the imaginary, [a] cliché in which historical realities and fantasies, visceral fears and contempt for all that is 'different' and 'alien' melt together." One can apply this same paradigm to the Roma's existence in present-day Romania as well. How we reached this point is a complicated question that warrants a clear analysis of the historical and economical underpinnings that influence its arrival. Pop-Curseu frames this question through the minority groups inhabiting early modern Europe, distilling his analysis into one essential summation to characterize the histrionic fear of the Other throughout this time period: "Jews in the West and Gypsies in the East." This statement makes it easy to understand how slogans like this one were militarized against particular groups of people. In the same light, Lucian Boia's formulation "The Romanians are neither Western nor Eastern. They lie between these two worlds" sheds considerable light on the question of situating the *us versus them* mentality in Romania's physical geography, along transnational borders that the

Roma are continuously shifting. Moving forward, my analysis of the Roma witch relies on Pop-Curseu's work to frame the attempt at excluding the Roma from Romanian society as a mode of Otherizing concomitant with the capitalist goals of a free market economy.

Given this, the 2011 witch tax is rationalized as an attempt to prove the existence of the Roma Witch Economy (WE) while also recognizing that its existence is best controlled through regulation and taxation. One way to interpret the tax, according to Mihaela Minca herself, is to celebrate it. Minca lauds the new law: "'This law is very good,'"…'It means that our magic gifts are recognized and I can open my own practice.'" This logic is deeply influenced by the capitalist motive that aims to justify any form existence—either animate or inanimate—by creating profit. In this logic, decisions are made on the basis of achieving the bottom line. Here, performing the witch identity makes its third and final authorization: authorizing Minca and her family witches to enter and participate in the European economy. Without performing this identity, Minca along with the Roma community continue to be excluded from participating and thriving in Romania's economy. Now, however, performing the witch identity is empowering because it permits a displaced group entry into the same economic market in which their participation is continuously measured.

On the other hand, it can also be deeply disempowering if we consider Ioana Szeman's argument that Roma are continually forced to "[perform] civility" in order to be taken seriously and allowed participation in mainstream culture. Here, the Roma are seen as performing the same "not us" gesture, which in turn, authorizes their participation and partial acceptance in mainstream culture. Regardless of which way we read it, this dynamic is held together by the witch identity.

Crafting and Gifting the Figure of the Witch

Until now, I've considered how the tax on general practitioners of magic and Roma witchcraft authorizes the Roma's participation in the mainstream European economy. Now, I turn to how this tax also creates a link between capitalism and the occult, and posits a new and exciting way that the Romanian government is seen to have fictively helped the Roma—by crafting and gifting them their own identity, that of the Roma witch, and by demonstrating that they're now accepted in mainstream society.

The logic of Minca's comment that the tax lends credibility to Roma witchcraft effectively links capitalism and the occult, positing itself as a new way to read active connections among the seemingly inflexible lines of state, profit, and occultism. After all, Minca's family, "Collected occult traditions and mixed them with their Orthodox faith," thus blending the spiritualism of the occult with that of the Christian. This reading also reveals a new link between the occult and the profit motive, suggesting how the occult can be carried out with the "bottom line" in mind. By creating the law, the Romanian government acknowledges this reading and adopts it as its thesis for creating the WE, an economy that needs to be controlled, as Milène Larsson reminds us, because of the "million Euros a year" profit the witches supposedly make.

The occult has fused with the secular scope of a post-Communist government, mediating the relationship between the two by creating a tax whose profits are directed to one party only. It's useful to place this assessment in conversation with Alexandra Cotofană's *Governing with Magic: Politics and Labors of the Occult in Romania*, which encapsulates this aim in its title alone. Cotofană is deeply concerned with how the spiritual and secular blend in Romania's post-communist economy. She addresses how many attempts at "governing with magic" are designed to re-assert Romania's once dubious global status: as of 2017, "Romania is EU's fastest growing economy." One way to read the witchcraft tax, then, is as an anxiety against communities that are not willing or able to continue developing Romania's competitive status.

Discussing the same tax, Cotofană writes, "One reason the politicians invoked for taxing labors of the occult has to do with modernity as an imagined passage of time, a rupture from an archaic, romanticized past: the practice is 'medieval', it delays 'modernization.'" Cotofană reads the tax as a way to modernize the "medieval," and thus bring the communities it's directed at into modernity. Although this dynamic is clearly what's happening in Romania today, the argument Cotofană identifies on behalf of the Romanian state is deeply one-sided, placing the Roma in competition with the state through the mediator that is taxation.

This reading also reveals another troubling layer of meaning: through this tax, the Romanian government is seen to have crafted and gifted the figure of the witch to the Roma, thus allowing them to perform a once illegal identity within the confines of a newly legal, regulated superstructure synonymous with the aims of the contemporary mainstream. By *crafting* and *gifting*, I invoke how the Romanian state uses the tax to authorize the profession of Roma witchcraft. This move positions the figure of the Roma witch as a gift to the Roma community, allowing them to practice a previously denied identity, now repurposed under the confines of contemporary fiscal regulation. *Essentially, by authorizing the existence and practice of Roma witchcraft, the Romanian government is seen to have built and given an identity to the Roma that the Roma already created and owned, that of the Roma witch.* "Governing with magic," thus takes on a completely new meaning, once again positioning Roma identity at the whims of the Romanian government who can tax, not tax, draw, and withdraw its authorization of this identity at any time. This move bolsters the government's ethos by placing them in a position as noble authorities that are willing and able to acknowledge new identities in the increasingly diverse country they inhabit. Ultimately, this move also extends an arm of reconciliation and redemption to the Roma—offering them, in other words, a pseudo introduction to modernity (which can be withdrawn at any time) by paying taxes.

It would be a mistake to claim this as evidence that the witch hunt has re-surfaced. Doing so delegitimates the physical violence women did experience during the early modern period. But it would be an equally serious mistake not to claim that the status of present-day Roma shares many similarities with the historical witch hunts cited at the beginning of this book. Today, the power dynamics have shifted, shedding the inefficiency of the witch hunt's older methods (physical violence and inquisition) in favor of our world's modernized concerns: taxes and the profit motive. The physical violence is gone—at least, in most communities, though violence against Roma is still present—replaced only with an updated concern: the bottom line and how best to achieve it.

The terror has been here all along. Consider Federici's argument that, "the witch hunt instituted a regime of terror on all women, from which emerged the new model of femininity to which women had to conform to be socially accepted in the developing capitalist society: sexless, obedient, submissive, resigned to subordination to the male world, accepting as natural the confinement to a sphere of activities that in capitalism has been completely devalued." Is this not what the Roma witches experience? Although they comfortably admit that their witchcraft allows them to transcend the "sexless, obedient, submissive" environments they inhabit while participating in it, are they not still submissive to the Romanian state, in one way or another, through fiscal legislation? What of the redemption and reconciliation narratives they're given—along with the figure of the witch—a figure that appears to have been *gifted* to them? Can't these also be read as moves to enforce the "obedient" and the "submissive"?

I pause for a moment to place this in conversation with the historical persecution the Roma have experienced. My goal in doing this is not to make equivalences between the physical violence women experienced during the early modern period as a result of practicing the same identity, but to demonstrate how violence against the Roma has for ages shared the same dynamics of power, submissiveness, and obedience, dynamics in turn, which have come to define women's position in capitalism today. In *The Roma in Romanian History*, Viorel Achim places Roma history in the context of persecution, identifying stages in their presence in Romania addled with deportation, eugenics, and physical violence. According to Achim, the "gypsy problem" originates in attempts made to integrate Roma into mainstream society, a process as plagued with inefficiencies and racist agendas in the twentieth century as it is now. Achim cites Ioan Facaoaru who led racist anti-gypsyism efforts across Romania:

> '…the process of assimilation is activated and aggravated not only by the large number of Gypsies, but also by other factors specific to the political conditions in Romania: the tolerant disposition of the Romanian people, the distribution of the Gypsies across the entirety of the country, the Gypsies' social promiscuity with the autochthonous population both in the towns and the villages, the existence of joint schools, the granting of land to many Gypsies, and the relaxation of sedentary living conditions, thereby facilitating their entry into the

Romanian community, the absence of any legal restrictions upon the Gypsies, and finally the indulgent attitude of the government and the administrative authorities towards them.'

The stage hosting these battles for assimilation and acculturation was often the human body. Adopting this "gypsy problem" in the 1940s, prime minister Ion Antonescu began the forced deportation of Roma to a work camp in Transnistria, a state at the time entwined in its own geographic squabbles with Moldova and the USSR.[1] In 1942, over 25,000 Roma "considered to be a 'problem'" were uprooted and moved to Transnistria. Conditions in the work camp were harsh, with "a large part of the Gypsy deportees in Transnistria [dying] of hunger, cold, disease and poverty," many plagued with the absolute "squalor" of their living conditions.

Given their history of persecution and the reality that the Romanian state is doing precious little beyond lip service to integrate the Roma into society, the Roma are still very much part of a confused system. The Roma witches, then, should not be seen as threats to capitalist modernity as they're typically presented because this reasoning competes with the reality that many Roma are severely unemployed. According to a report titled "Poverty and Employment: The Situation of Roma in 11 EU Member States" produced by the European Union Agency

---

1   According to Achim, "none of Antonescu's orders with regard to the Gypsies bore his signature and none of them were published either in the Official Gazette or elsewhere. The orders were given verbally to ministers and transmitted to the General Inspectorate of the Gendarmeries for execution." This says a great deal about the political climate surrounding this decision, as well as Antonescu's suspicion, later confirmed, that the deportation was extremely unpopular with the Romanian mainstream.

for Fundamental Rights, "About 90% of Roma in the survey have an income below the national poverty threshold; about 40% of the children live in households struggling with malnutrition or hunger." In employment, "only 28% of Roma and 45% of non-Roma living nearby aged 16 and above indicate paid work as their main activity." In Romania, specifically, 29% of Roma self-reported "paid work"[2] as their "main activity status" whereas this figure is closer to 40% for non-Roma status.

It would not be a stretch to suggest that the 16% income tax on Roma witches would debilitate the WE in general as well as its individual practitioners. As one witch points out, "'What is there to tax, when we hardly earn anything?'" The same article cites that "payments to witches and astrologers usually are small, the equivalent of $7 to $10, and made with cash." Although the article uses this detail as a reason why the tax would be difficult to enforce, it neglects to mention how these witches' livelihoods depend on small monetary contributions like this one. Minca herself relies on non-taxable payments from her clients submitted through Western Union and MoneyGram.

Evading the tax is also a method of feminist protest against the mainstream which continually rejects the Roma's existence. It ensures that they're not forced to surrender their profits to a state doing hardly enough to reintegrate them into society. The WE is a microeconomy predicted on the freelance labor of witches who transcend the celebrity/noncelebrity status that Minca and Bratara share as a result of their notoriety and exposure. It is these individual practitioners that the witch tax would ultimately disenfranchise and dislocate from future participation in the larger macroeconomy.

---

2   This figure includes "full-time, part-time, ad hoc jobs, [and] self-employment" statuses.

At the same time, the law is also a troubling representation of the Roma as Other because it forces them to pay a fee for being cultural practitioners of their own, previously-denied heritage. As a group already forced to recast their own nomadism into forms that are more compatible with the Western world, today's Roma are effectively barred from existence in most economic industries. They are repeatedly denied working opportunities by the pervasive stereotypes that have been militarized against them. This has led advocates to coin the term antigypyism, or the "the specific racism towards Roma, Sinti, Travelers and others who are stigmatized as 'gypsies' in the public imagination."[3] According to the Alliance Against Antigypsyism, antigypsyism, "operates on the basis of the projection of certain shared traits that supposedly diverge from common norms, while denying those affected the recognition of personal or common dignity." These include the popular stereotypes that gypsies are lazy, ineffective workers, desperately wanting government assistance without demonstrating any work ethic as the "hooligans and unemployed." Often, their physical appearance is attacked and they are vilified for the cleanliness of their bodies (see Voicu's comments cited earlier in this book). This analysis helps us understand how antigypsyism is a perva-

---

3   According to the Alliance Against Antigypsyism, "we have deliberately chosen the notation without hyphen: "antigypsyism"; not "anti-G(g)ypsyism". This is because the latter would inadvertently give the impression that something like 'gypsyism' exists. Although certain currents of thought assert the existence of Rromanipen—a shared frame of affiliation among Roma—this should not be considered at all related to the projections pronounced in anti-gypsyist discourse.... What those who embody antigypsyism are antagonistic towards is actually a creation of the collective imagination that is entirely ignorant of Romani cultures and perspectives."

sive enterprise that attacks the economic, political, and moral spheres of Romanian consciousness—both as that consciousness seeks to represent and to exclude the Roma. The witch tax is another, repurposed form of this institutionalized antigypsyism because it ultimately asks Roma witches to pay for entrance and participation in their own culture while the mainstream culture writ large collects these witches' profits. These profits, it's easy to assume, are then used for the collective benefit of the non-Roma who themselves deliberately exclude the Roma on whose backs these advances have been made. At its most basic level, this form of economic racism celebrates the advancement of expensive superhighways, for instance, while refusing to acknowledge that many Roma still drive horses and buggies.[4]

Grappling with the Imaginary: Racist Roma Witch Representations

It is from Pop-Curseu's figuration of Roma witches as a "great [constraint] of the imaginary, [a] cliché in which historical realities and fantasies, visceral fears and contempt for all that is 'different' and 'alien' melt together" that most popular, ahistorical representations of these witches are born. Aside from the genuine witches interviewed in the *Vice News* film, one should not exempt the popular news media from this ahistoricism. This ahistoricisim is present in many avenues of culture, and will continue casting its shadow over the mythology being produced about the Roma.

---

4   Autostrada Soarelui or the "Sun's Motorway," is one famous example of a technological achievement built and celebrated for "the people" without acknowledging that many Roma do not have the economic means to own a vehicle in the first place.

In its article, "Romanian Witches Cast Dark Spells on Government in Tax Protest," *Foreign Policy Magazine* falls victim to this same representational faux pas, thereby allowing a mainly American audience to revel in the racist clichés of anti-gypsyism. The article, which covers the aforementioned witch tax, includes the following cover image:

Oliver Lang AFP/Getty Images 1

The dynamics of this image are clearly intended to convey the representational, stereotypical figure of the early modern witch dwelling in our consciousness—every detail from the exaggerated noses to the explicitly ugly figuration of the mostly female bodies is designed to be grotesque. Of the five witches in the image's foreground, each has no more than one tooth, a gaping mouth, and a pair of deliberately bastardized (even racialized) lips. The faces themselves appear as though destroyed by physical violence: the teeth have been presumably knocked out, the facial features rearranged and reconstructed, and the eyes impacted—all by violent force and bludgeoned trauma, one assumes, in the typical witch narrative, either as the reason these women became witches and/or the punishment for doing so. From this image alone, it's clear what a solid, mass disseminated representation of contemporary witchcraft must include. (*Foreign Policy Magazine*, it's important to note, lauds an annual 91 million "annual page views" and 900,000 "newsletter subscribers.")

Unfortunately, a Google Images search returns a link to a Party City set of witch costumes, a Pinterest board, and a page on *Halloween Express*. The article's author may not have intended perfect historical accuracy, but a genuine photo of Roma witchcraft would have done better rhetorical work for their cause.[5]

In this tradition, the Roma are presented as Others twice over: they are first barred from participation in the mainstream Romanian economy; more damagingly, arguably, they are barred from themselves, inhibited from acting as practitioners of a self-created identity. Instead, they are subsumed into ahistorical presentations such as the image cited above, presentations that reach a much larger audience than many Roma would ever envision. They are forced to inhabit the clichéd stereotypes that have forever been used to dominate them, subjugating them into a larger superstructure whose own wealth is predicated on their hard work. Pop-Curseu's "visceral fears and contempt for all that is 'different' and 'alien'" really do "melt together," but in an ahistorical presentation designed to dominate the Roma

---

5   Interestingly, the author of this article concedes, "The photo above is of German witches. I couldn't find any Romanian witch photos."

through subjugation which begins at the linguistic level and ends at the national, economic one.

Yet the extent to which this subjugation is recognized by those who enact it is incredible. Politicians like Popoviciu, who maintain an active fear of witchcraft and allow it to drive their fiscal and legislative policy, may acknowledge the existence of witches and the occult spiritualism they define, but they do so at the privilege of sitting on the side of the desk almost entirely unaffected by the legislation it creates. The group of people who define this dynamic, a dynamic that implicitly acknowledges its hegemonic existence by genuinely believing in the threat of Roma witchcraft, and then driving home in their luxury cars to a separate, off-camera reality, is partially to blame for the status of today's Roma. This group's success—we're led to believe by their on-camera presence—contributes to the double otherizing of the Roma because (and not as a consequence) they are able to project beyond it by starring in television roles that celebrate witchcraft such as those produced by *Vice News*. What marks their guilt in this debate is the privilege to choose which side they stand on without facing the consequences of that economic reality. Yet it would be reductive of me to suggest that politicians of this consciousness are ultimately to blame for the double otherized status of the Roma witches. Instead, as is the case in many cultural matters, a complex interplay of issues, people, and agendas are ultimately to blame. If this interplay is to be reconciled, and the Roma are ever to be elevated and fully integrated, it behooves all groups across the divide to understand how a productive plan for the future includes studying the failures of the past.

Moving Forward

One wonders, then, what a future built on productively including the Roma into mainstream culture would look like. What would it look like if, as Pop-Curseu posits, "Contemporary witches [really did] enrich themselves at the expense of the gullible and build villas with underground garages for the luxury cars they own?" To most Romanians, this question is still absurd, and will probably remain absurd, because of the entrenched presentation of the Roma throughout Romanian history. Recent reclamations of Roma identity such as the success against the witch tax will lead the way for a new integration of the Roma first into the economic sphere of existence and eventually the cultural one as well, but these are not without their own problems. This success begins at the level of small transactions inside a microeconomy, but blossoms with mass representations like the *Vice News* film that will continue to push the Roma witch into the foreground of Romanian consciousness. Today, this consciousness has made it more difficult to ignore the Roma's existence as a displaced group that is now learning to operate in the same structure that has continually worked to defeat it. Although this move of empowerment shouldn't be read as a complete separation from the mainstream's dominance, it should be rationalized as a move of support now that the rest of the world is listening and starting to fight back.

Conclusion

Summation

In this book, I've suggested that witchcraft is continually involved in a transaction of authority and authorizes a series of identities and actions, including but not limited to the authorization of Roma identity, female identity, and capitalist identity. I've presented each of these identities through film, and have discussed how the platform sponsoring this film also interacts with the transaction of authority.

I've argued that witchcraft authorizes Roma identity. By performing the roles and actions of traditional European witchcraft, Roma witches are seen to enter a culture with a lineage extending past the national mythology that grips Romania so strongly. This performance serves as a mechanism to ensure the survival of Roma culture because it allows them to distance themselves through "not us" gesturing. The Roma thus perform what it means to be a Romanian citizen. This is made possible by performing witchcraft.

I've also argued that witchcraft authorizes female identity. It does this by suggesting that Roma witches should be seen as strong women who can carry out both good and evil. The witches I profile admit this, and use this tacit acknowledgement to foreground their performance of witchcraft in the *Vice News* film. Performing witchcraft allows these women to be taken seriously, to be heard, to be listened to, and to be feared. In this respect, witchcraft is framed as a feminist identity, a move of empowerment for a community who is often (and strategically) disempowered by both the non-Roma mainstream and the Romanian government.

Finally, I've argued that witchcraft authorizes capitalist identity. It does this by giving the Roma a platform on which to transact monetary business. For the witches profiled in this book, this carries distinct fiscal success. From the basis of this fiscal success, I argue that witchcraft authorizes capitalist identity, allowing Roma women one avenue to enter the European economy, which has often barred them from participation while deploying racist stereotypes to fault them for not trying hard enough. On one hand, this encourages the Romanian government to celebrate their efforts at inclusion. On the other, it carries the acknowledgement that proposed legislation including the tax on witches and practitioners of the occult are yet additional ways to displace and silence a once-disempowered community. The Roma witch is thus involved in a complex transaction between stereotype, mythology, and profit, enmeshed in all three of these dynamics, while also gaining distinct fiscal and cultural success as a result.

Future Perspectives, Or,
The Witchcraft Economy Lives On

The thrust of my argument has been that witchcraft authorizes non-white, non-male, non-capitalist Roma individuals living in Romania. By doing so, it also empowers them to see themselves as members of the Romanian state, as individuals with "actual citizenship" who can contend with the non-Roma main-stream. *Vice News* authorizes this move, asserting an argument of acceptance supported by a wealthy, powerful American news mogul with far-reaching exposure in the global world.

In the space that remains, I answer a few anticipated objections to my argument and then motion toward the future of Roma witchcraft in both Romania and the European Union.

1. *Rather than relying on the occult, a dubious, only now profit-able industry, the Roma should turn to "legitimate" professions and focus on educating generations of citizens for traditional jobs in the European economy.* This argument has always been around in both Roma and non-Roma communities. At its core, it relies on delegitimating the occult, arguing that what is real and what is legitimate include tradition-al professions such as doctors, lawyers, and teachers. This argument almost always neglects to mention how these high-power, sometimes high-paying professions are also traditionally reserved for white men. Until we can estab-lish a political and economic reality and until we can grant Roma both legal and "actual citizenship," it will remain strategically difficult for them to enter these high-power professions. Even then, this argument will need to contend with the fact that the occult and the figure of the witch are both "having a moment" as Kristen Sollée argues. They are both our future. As with so many other things foisted onto millennials' shoulders, this dynamic will force them to find new (and profitable) ways to make the most of our newly forged occult interests. It would be a mistake to deny and delegitimate the future profitability of the occult.

2. *Magic and the occult are incompatible with our world's increasing push toward pragmatic, science-driven professions. As a result, they are useless, non-contributors to the future of human culture.* Again, when this argument surfaces, it tends to (deliberately) neglect mentioning how the occult serves to empower groups traditionally excluded from science-driven professions. It also subscribes to our world's obsession with pragmatism, arguing from the basis that what separates the useful from the useless is how well it can be commodified, scaled, and marketed. Of course, the figure of the witch can (and probably) will need to contend with these forces in the future. But as Tituba in *I Tituba, The Black Witch of Salem* reminds us, "'Everyone gives [the] word [witch] a different meaning. Everyone believes he can fashion a witch to his way of thinking so that she will satisfy his ambitions, dreams, and desires.'" The identity will be used, reused, fashioned, refashioned, and empowered in our future.

3. *Vice News should be celebrated for giving exposure to Roma women, using their platform of global coverage to portray the lives and struggles these women face with the rest of the world.* Yes, and no. It would be a mistake not to celebrate *Vice* for spending time listening, filming, and broadcasting the lives of Roma witches to the global world. But it would be an equally serious mistake not to approach their representation skeptically, and to evaluate how their representation engages with or diverges from Roma stereotypes. Not doing so would subscribe to the often-voiced argument about representation that any representation of minority groups is good representation. This cannot be determined without an informed analysis of the ideological work carried out by any representation. I hope I've laid out my argument for the

reader to evaluate and then come to their own conclusion about Roma representation in this film.

It would be difficult to estimate the cost—and thus, in capitalism's eyes—the legitimacy of the Roma Witchcraft Economy. As I've suggested, it's somewhat hasty to value it yearly at "one million euros" as Larsson does in "Casting Curses and Love Spells." But from the anxiety spent legislating this economy through tax, it's clear that the profession of the Roma witch is either being legitimated or disempowered. The future of the Witchcraft Economy will contend with this realization, arguing for acceptance from the basis that some witches have now entered the capitalist market and, what's more, are thriving. Ultimately, I view any anxiety over the success of the Witchcraft Economy as an anxiety about the status of strong women in society. This anxiety is as old as history; it rationalizes itself by obsessively monitoring, controlling, and legislating women's bodies and actions. As Silvia Federici has suggested, this is also an anxiety over the purpose of human reproduction in capitalism. In this argument, women, who serve to reproduce the future of the workforce, will now become distracted by the occult, and if the film I analyze is any indication, seriously distracted. Thus, it will be useful to consider not only the monetization of the Witchcraft Economy, but how this newly legitimated profession serves to distract and even distance women from the traditional roles history has written them into. I'm partially optimistic that this will be empowering—that the witch will continue as a "Feminist Symbol" as the *New York Times* casts it. But it would be a mistake not to attune ourselves to how framing the occult as a distraction for future empowered women will also allow the majority to continue clamping down and legislating the status of strong women in society. What will this look like in twenty years? We can only venture a guess given witches' place in society today. It is within this view that the most productive assessments of witchcraft will take place.

The Fairy Tale and the
Aesthetics of Ugliness

The Roma witches profiled in this book represent one iteration of what it means to adopt the identity of the witch. There are many more. The following essay evaluates the relationship between ugliness and witchcraft, seeking to answer why ugly women were often thought to be witches. This is as true historically as it is today.

O Princess Dulcinea, lady of this captive heart,
a grievous wrong hast thou done me to drive me
forth with scorn, and with inexorable obduracy
banish me from the presence of thy beauty.

—Miguel de Cervantes Saavedra, *Don Quixote*

Let's get ugly.

—Ugly Duck Coffee, Rochester, NY

In classical and contemporary scholarship alike, ugliness is often imagined as the opposite of beauty. According to Edmund Burke, beauty is "that quality or those qualities in bodies, by which they cause love, or some passion similar to it" whereas ugliness, he imagines, "to be in all respects the opposite to those qualities which we have laid down for the constituents of beauty." But this binary opposition does not account for the genuine struggles of the group to which it is usually ascribed and then used against: women. The gendering of ugliness and the socio-political consequences this carries is worthy of academic scholarship because it necessitates an analysis of how ugliness has been used and abused against women, specifically those of the early modern period, a time that defined itself by its obsession with the concerns of women 'on the outside,' women who practiced magic, and even women who were thought to be witches. These categories often melted together, revealing an anxiety over the status of women in society, which are all encapsulated in the early modern witch hunt, a distinctly hysterical (and male) reaction to the figure of the witch, what Rita

Voltmer characterizes as "the disorderly 'other', a rebel against patriarchal, social, political, and religious order."[1] The task of evaluating the popular representations of witches that many people would have read and understood at this time, however, typically means studying the male hysterical misogyny of the *Malleus maleficarum* or *Hammer of Witches*, arguably the most famous text on witchcraft, but a text that scholars are "uncertain [about] how much it encouraged witch-hunting." Later writers including Jean Bodin would position the witch as a threat "to the state and the public," but these writings only implicate an older, typically well-read audience whose impressionability, although heightened in a time of mass hysteria like the witch hunt, is questionable at best.

Contemporary scholarship into the conflation of ugliness and witchcraft, what I will refer to as Ugly Scholarship, has failed to move beyond these traditional, characteristically 'witchy' texts. It is undeniable that femininity, ugliness, and witchcraft are deeply connected. It is equally undeniable that the traditional texts in this discipline should be studied with scholarly precision as the primary sources they are, but what I suggest in this essay is that it is nearly impossible to articulate the place of 'witchy' women in society (especially strong women, often reduced to the status of witch) without also considering how this place is mediated through the dynamic of ugliness. Ugliness, I will argue, is strategically used to empower and disempower, to embody and disembody the female witches it depicts, who are seen as a threat to the world order of the text they inhabit. Attempting to do this solely by studying primary documents such as the *Malleus* and implicating their well-read,

---

1   See Ronald Hutton's *The Witch: A History of Fear from Ancient Times to the Present* for a comprehensive, contemporary analysis of the early modern witch hunt.

erudite audience ultimately reveals a shortcoming in contemporary scholarship. To better understand the association between femininity, ugliness, and witchcraft, we must pay attention to an often-forgotten audience, children and young adults, and to the texts primarily designed for their consumption, fairy tales. Doing so acknowledges this genre's socializing goal while also arguing that its intended audience has the most time at its disposal to move beyond the damaging attitudes that consider femininity, ugliness, and witchcraft as one.

The fairy tales of the Brothers Grimm create a strong association among these three categories, which are strategically deployed in an effort to socialize readers (primarily young children and students) into a world that connects ugliness with fear—regardless of the physical pain 'ugly' characters must undergo to prove otherwise. This association is effected through the figure of the witch, a container for the general ills of any society. In these tales, the witch is afforded a privileged position—however unwilling readers and writers are to admit—as a pedagogical figure used (and abused) ad nauseam. This pedagogical project is not radically different from that of the Fairy Tale proper, which, as theorist Jack Zipes maintains, "operate[s] ideologically to indoctrinate children so that they will conform to dominant social standards that are not necessarily established in their behalf." A detailed study of Grimm's tales with these questions in mind will generate new insights into the presentations and representations of witches in the early modern period, and the consequences of these representations, even if the Brothers Grimm are writing their *Kinder-und Hausmärchen*, or the *Children's and Household Tales* between 1812 and 1815, roughly 330 years after the publication of Kramer's *Malleus*.

Two character archetypes dominate the tales. The first, the ugly-woman-as-witch, asserts that a woman's ugliness contributes (if not completely, then significantly) to her labelling as a witch. Being a witch means being on the outside of many things, one of which is conventional beauty. Beauty, which indeed poses a threat to the world order of these tales, is still less terrifying than complete ugliness, which is strategically used by the world of the text to socialize young readers into fearing the Ugly, and by convenient extension, the Other. It must be noted that this archetype makes it possible for a woman to be a witch without practicing a form of distinct, stereotypical magic or spellcasting. A woman is a witch if she is relegated, both physically and/or figuratively, to the outside of society; if she inspires a vague, unexplainable sense of fear in the people around her; if, while on the outside of that society, she gains access to something typically seen as a scarcity; and finally, if she is completely at odds with the beauty standards of her world: labeled 'ugly.'

The second, the witch-as-ugly-woman, emboldens the first. The witch represents a perverted beauty, either one that has faded with age or violence. She is scary, the tales argue, because she is ugly; she is ugly, they maintain, because she is scary. Even in their imagination today, young children find it difficult to conceive of an evil person who is not ugly—who is not simultaneously on the outside of both beauty and goodness. This association, I will argue, originates in the fairy tales, a genre designed by adults to teach other adults the morals required of their society. In the eighteenth century, this project is applied to children.[2]

Through separate readings of "Rapunzel" and "Hansel and Gretel," I assert that the world of beauty and ugliness these tales represent engages in an interplay with the ugly-woman-as-witch archetype, a pedagogic project we've yet to escape in

---

2   See Zipes' *Fairy Tales and the Art of Subversion* (2012).

today's world where ugliness is simultaneously tolerated yet still presented as a lesson of fear. Reclaiming ugliness, both as a social and economic move of empowerment, as Ugly Duck Coffee does, is critically important to the future of Ugly Scholarship because it pushes past the hysteria dominating traditional understandings of ugliness and reveals a host of topics[3] we will need to grapple with in the future. Who thought ugliness could be so fashionable?

Ugly Scholarship

The position of Ugly Scholarship as a subcategory of Aesthetics—as the latter relates to questions of beauty and representation—is best credited to Karl Rosenkranz, whose compendious *Aesthetics of Ugliness* provides an analysis encapsulated in the radical proposition "An aesthetics of ugliness? And why not?" Rosenkranz deconstructs the notion of ugliness as "inseparable from the concept of beauty, since the one contains the other in its development as perpetual aberration." He enumerates the various categories of ugliness, going so far as to propose that "In the concept of the human, thus, there is no ugliness," a contention I will have more to say about later on. His most striking conclusion, one not out of keeping with his central aim, is his association between "real beauty" and freedom: "Without freedom, thus, no real beauty; without unfreedom or constraint,

---

3   Among others, these necessitate a discussion of the dynamic interplay between beauty and the capitalism. Beauty, which has always been marketable, must now compete with ugliness, which is clearly marketed by businesses like Ugly Duck Coffee, an espresso bar that has received local, even national news (see Food and Wine's 2018 article "The Best Coffee in Every State").

no real ugliness," framing the question of beauty and ugliness through freedom. To Rosenkranz, ugliness or "real ugliness," is a question of "unfreedom," even "constraint" within some larger superstructure; this definition will be useful to my considerations of femininity and witchcraft, two superstructures that present themselves as modes of empowerment for the women who engage in them, yet are co-extensively vilified and demonized by the culture they operate in. The delicacy with which he distinguishes between beauty and "real beauty," ugliness and "real ugliness" suggests a clear dichotomy between ugliness as a transgression of conventional beauty and a new form of ugliness designed to be strategically used against a specific group of people. According to this logic, witchcraft involves the acknowledgement and reclamation of ugliness from the bounds of freedom and unfreedom. Neither the sorceress in "Rapunzel" nor the witch in "Hansel and Gretel" succeed as they are both ultimately destroyed and forgotten.

Rosenkranz's reliance on freedom may not be unfounded in contemporary aesthetics, but it is at odds with traditional formulations of beauty and ugliness as questions of internality which implicate the soul. In the *Enneads*, Plotinus asserts that "an ugly soul" is "dissolute, unjust, teeming with lusts, torn by inner discord, beset by craven fears and petty envies. It thinks indeed. But it thinks only of the perishable and the base." He ascribes the soul thinking and feeling capabilities but maintains that it thinks "only of the perishable and the base," two aspects defined by their transience in the same way that beauty is. To Plotinus, beauty is fleeting whereas ugliness—especially ugliness of the soul, which he considers more serious than external ugliness—is eternal. As conventional beauty fades with age and is replaced by ugliness, the soul itself becomes impure: "the soul is ugly when it is not purely itself," suggesting a relationship between the purity of one's soul and one's outward appearance. Even more radically, however, Plotinus associates ugliness with evil: "Ought we not say that this ugliness has come to it as an evil from without, soiling it, rendering it filthy, 'encumbering it' with turpitude of every sort, so that it no longer has an activity or sensation that is clean?" This association blends the language of sanitation and purity ("soiling," "filthy," "clean") with the language of morality ("turpitude," "encumbering," and the presumption that the human needs to be made "clean" to be beautiful). This rhetoric links ugliness and evil now that evil, which is already a question of internality, has been fused with ugliness, a question of visible externality.

Why, then, should we be interested in The Ugly given its ability to wholly corrupt the body and soul? In *Poetics*, Aristotle identifies the distinct pleasure we experience by engaging with The Ugly, framing it in response to the inherent human drive for mimesis:

> [W]e enjoy looking at the most accurate representations of things which in themselves we find painful to see, such as the forms of the lowest animals and of corpses. The reason for this is that learning is a very great pleasure, not only for philosophers, but for other people as well.… They enjoy seeing images because they learn as they look at them, and reason out what each thing is.

The notion that we derive pleasure from what we "find painful to see" is distinctly pedagogic. It privileges learning as "great pleasure" both to the philosopher and the common man, setting forth a proto-Rousseauian argument on the status of education in society that will be later adopted by fairy tale scholars like Jack Zipes. We're drawn to the painful in and of itself because it teaches us, presenting in opposition to what we are usually taught with: the beautiful and the good. We're drawn to the diseased, the "lowest animals" and "corpses" because they represent the perverted beauty so often presented in opposition to ourselves. This sheds light on the witch-as-ugly-woman archetype: the witch must be ugly to serve the pedagogic function of the fairy tale at large and to inculcate a fear in the same objects Aristotle presents as fascination. Yet this view does not account for the status of ugliness and evil, which become nearly indistinguishable in Rosenkranz's *Aesthetics*.

Rosenkranz's scholarship categorizes the evil of ugliness and the ugliness of evil into three separate domains: the criminal, the ghastly, and the diabolical, allowing him to conclude that "The evil will is the ethically ugly," an argument not far away from Plotinus' stance on "[the] ugly soul." In his introduction on evil, Rosenkranz qualifies: "One should not thus await here a treatise on the concept of evil; this belongs to ethics; *aesthetics has to assume it*, busying itself with the form of the phenomenon, insofar as the same is capable of expressing morally ugly content."[4] In other words, any aesthetics of ugliness must begin by assuming that a representation of evil is synonymous with a representation of ugliness. We can expect this conclusion given the nineteenth century world Rosenkranz is writing in, a world that saw the proliferation of physiognomy, whose central failure was its very thesis that "the science of physiognomy with discernment could read the internal from the external, the character of humankind from the countenance." It's easy to see how the ugly and the evil operate together inside the frame physiognomy provides. Johann Kaspar Lavater's 1775 *Physiognomische Fragmente zur Beförderung der Menschenkenntnis und Menschenliebe*, or *Physiognomic Fragments for the Advancement of the Knowledge and the Love of Man*, which brought physiogno-

---

4 My italics.

my into the late eighteenth century, gives credence to Rosenk-ranz's later speculations on the association between evil and ug-liness: "It is just as true that ugliness in and for itself is identical with evil, namely insofar as evil is the radical, the absolute, the ethically and religiously ugly." Positioning evil as "radical" al-lows him considerable creative freedom to speculate and even-tually theorize on the systematicity of ugliness, to propose, for instance, a discrete model of categorizing ugliness; today, such a system seems maligned given the ways visible appearances have been used against those who didn't—either out of choice or force—conform with them.

Rosenkranz further diverges from Plotinus' stance that "ug-liness has come to it as an evil from without, soiling it, ren-dering it filthy, 'encumbering it' with turpitude of every sort" by acknowledging that Plotinus' assertion is implicitly flawed because it extends the association between ugliness and evil too far. Whereas Plotinus is quick to blend the language of sanita-tion with that of morality, thereby connecting the "soiling" and the "filthy" with Rosenkranz's theory of moral evil based on physical appearance, Rosenkranz cautions that this connection may be academically fruitful, but can be socially dangerous be-cause it's easily misused: "If one however stretches this identity so far that the cause of the ugly in general is supposed to lie in evil, that is an overloading of its concept, which inevitably must lead to untrue and violent abstractions." He proposes that al-though "ugliness in and for itself is identical with evil," we must refrain from drawing direct causal relationships by our instinct to "[stretch] this identity so far." This dynamic contradiction—insofar as one can call it that—will foreground my analysis of the ugly-woman-as-witch and the witch-as-ugly-woman, two archetypes whose distinctions are frequently (and strategically) blurred to produce similar results.

Ugly Women and Witchcraft

Why must the witch be an ugly woman? I am tempted to ask another, even more historically salient question, Why must the ugly woman be a witch? Casting someone as 'ugly' is an undeniable method of social control. The ugly woman, also figured as the witch in many early modern societies, is outcasted because she is ugly and is ugly because she is thought evil. Often, this evil is the result of simple male confusion and curiosity, which easily mutate into speculations on evil. It is no mistake, for instance, that the question of why there are more female witches than male witches appears early on in *Malleus*:

> As for the first question, why a greater number of witches is found in the fragile feminine sex than among men….For some learned men propound this reason; that there are three things in nature, the Tongue, an Ecclesiastic, and a Woman, which know no moderation in goodness or vice….they have slippery tongues, and are unable to conceal from the fellow-women those things which by evil arts they know; and, since they are weak, they find an easy and secret manner of vindicating themselves by witchcraft….Therefore a wicked woman is by her nature quicker to waver in her faith, and consequently quicker to abjure the faith, which is the root of witchcraft.[5]

The abjuration of faith, cited as the "root of witchcraft" along with a wavering "in her faith" assumes, first and foremost, that the subject is female. Male faith is present by default. Aside from its blatant disregard for factual evidence, the most damaging aspect of this misogyny is the absolutism used to articulate it. Kramer takes no opportunity to make a moral, even ethical qualification because doing so is at odds with the larger argument he's making. In lieu of a qualified character judgement

---

5   See Part I Question IV.

based on evidence, *Malleus*—along with the larger tradition it creates and operates in—isolates the physical, the "slippery tongues" and "evil arts" that are to blame for feminine indiscretions rather than considering the serious, often elevated position these women occupy in their culture.

Integrating *Malleus* with Rosenkranz's thesis that "Without freedom, thus, no real beauty; without unfreedom or constraint, no real ugliness" suggests that the freedom Rosenkranz sees as a necessary pre-condition for beauty must be denied *automatically* from the witches' realm of experience for their manufactured identity to function. If they cannot be beautiful, Rosenkranz argues, they cannot be free. This circular argument is ultimately most damaging for women, who find themselves trapped inside a larger cyclical superstructure of power designed to simultaneously defeat them and sadistically encourage them to keep trying. The ugly woman must be the witch of any particular society because it is a convenient method of control, of positioning Voltmer's "disorderly 'other'" within the confines of her oppressors who can continue to exert social control over her. Labeling and denouncing her makes it easier to justify removing and vilifying her for the central project of any witch hunt. Finally, once a woman is cast as 'ugly,' it's nearly impossible for her to reclaim any identity beyond that; this allows the mainstream to continue using her as a puppet for whichever pedagogic mission it is engaged in. The fairy tale genre exploits this logic ad infinitum.

"Rapunzel" and Manufactured Ugliness

"Rapunzel" is a story that manufactures ugliness from evil. The "sorceress" of the tale becomes evil after she impedes the Prince's access to Rapunzel's body by confining her to the tower. It is too tempting to read "Rapunzel" as a tale about the frailties of youth and beauty, which was surely intended for the young audience these tales are designed for, and to completely sideline a more productive reading of the figure of the witch in this tale, a woman whose inherent concerns with the society she inhabits are suspended in favor of a Romantic reading that privileges the *Sturm und Drang* of early adolescence.

We are never told that the sorceress in "Rapunzel" is ugly; even the rhetorical space she receives pales in comparison with the evil manufactured from her actions. At the beginning of the tale, we learn that the beautiful vegetable garden she owns, in which her rapunzel lettuce grows, is "surrounded by a high wall" that "nobody dared enter...because it belonged to a sorceress who was very powerful and feared by all." We are *told* she is "very powerful" and "feared by all," but these statements seem hollow since the sorceress does not physically harm any of the characters in the tale. In fact, it's difficult to see the sorceress as evil since she charitably promises the husband and wife unlimited lettuce to satisfy the wife's cravings so long as they pledge their first-born baby to her. But she is not beautiful—and cannot be beautiful—in Burke's traditional definition. She does not embody "those qualities in bodies, by which they cause love, or some passion similar to it." In fact, she actively works to corrupt the young love interests of Rapunzel and the Prince. In the binary opposition of Burke's definition, she is ugly, "opposite to those qualities which we have laid down for the constituents of beauty" because the tale is designed to highlight her inhibition of the Prince's love rather than her own suffering at the hands of the dominant culture.

The sorceress becomes evil in the mythic imagination surrounding the tale. In lieu of any tremendous, physical evil, the witch's appearance is used as the central vehicle for transmitting her perceived evil: the tale cannot operate "ideologically" to use Jack Zipes' words, if the witch is not presented as evil as a result of her ugliness. The sentimentality of the tale conveniently assumes that she is also ugly because she never had a chance to fulfill the project of the bourgeois family with a spouse and child. Rather than presenting a reading of "Rapunzel" as a story of adolescent love, which is certainly in line with the "ideological" operation of the tale in popular consciousness, I contend that it is a story of nascent motherhood, a story whose deeply feeling "sorceress" if we can even call her that, is ostracized for not having children of her own; this ideological reading is complicated by the fact that she does want to have children, demonstrating this by trapping Rapunzel in the tower, which represents a perverted form of maternal protection. The sorceress protects Rapunzel, the central object of beauty in the tale, by treating her like another stock of lettuce, physically sheltering her with the same methods she uses to protect her vegetable garden because this is the only method of protection she knows how to use. The logic of the tale forces the sorceress to choose between motherhood, which she desperately wants to experience, and the prospect of being conventionally beautiful; in the logic of the tale, she cannot have both. When she grasps at both, which the pedagogic function of the fairy tale forces her to do, she becomes ugly—ostracized by and for her failed appearance and failed aspirations at motherhood.

Yet this explanation does not account for how the sorceress' ugliness is militarized against her. It also doesn't do justice to Rosenkranz's thesis of how ugliness and evil are one in our collective imagination, presumably leading the children who read the fairy tale to the same conclusion. To reconcile these difficulties, we must consider the sorceress' paramount act of social evil, her removal of Rapunzel's beautiful hair. Though tempting to also blame the sorceress for the Prince's fate after he jumps from the tower having realized that Rapunzel's hair has deceived him, this reading assumes an agency the sorceress doesn't have. In fact, the only object the sorceress does control (even Rapunzel's body is outside her control once she reaches the age of sexual maturity), is Rapunzel's hair, which becomes intangible (and thus controllable) after it's cut off. Before the sorceress removes Rapunzel's hair, Grimm characterize her as "very powerful" and "feared by all," formidable but rhetorically empty representations of the social evil she's actually thought to embody in the mythic imagination of the tale. She's said to have "an angry look" when she first meets the husband stealing her lettuce, a characterization seemingly absent of genuine fear, but one that sets in motion the association between her ugliness and the evil she's about to fulfill.

In her single act of violence, the sorceress removes the embodiment (and work) of Rapunzel's twenty years of demonstrable beauty, her hair:

> In her fury she seized Rapunzel's beautiful hair, wrapped it around her left hand several times, grabbed a pair of scissors with her right hand, and *snip snap* the hair was cut off, and the beautiful braids lay on the ground. Then the cruel sorceress took Rapunzel to a desolate land where she had to live in great misery and grief.

It's significant that the sorceress acts with "fury," the first (and only) example of violent anger, even rage that she will demonstrate in the tale. In a dynamic reversal, this moment represents how the ugliness that has been so strongly used against the sorceress is now militarized against Rapunzel herself, the object of maternal desire that the sorceress must wrest from the more likely candidate for the girl's own desire, the Prince: the sorceress *becomes* evil (she is already figured as ugly) by robbing Rapunzel of the central tenet of her own beauty, which represents something the witch desires, but does not, cannot, and should not have according to the logic of the tale. She responds by disembodying Rapunzel as an act of jealous revenge against the girl *and* the larger structure of the tale now that she's realized that she can no longer shelter the girl from the adolescent sexuality that is literally climbing up her wall. But this is also an act of social evil because it seeks to destroy something that the sorceress has worked so hard to manufacture and control, Rapunzel's hair, and by extension her beauty. The sorceress becomes evil not by sheltering Rapunzel from the complexities of nascent sexuality—it is inevitable, after all, that sexuality wins—but by destroying the beauty she's worked so diligently to manufacture by keeping Rapunzel physically locked out of the same adolescent experience central to many of the tales.[6] Readers who realize this also realize the lengths the sorceress has gone not only to ensure Rapunzel and the Prince do not interact, but also to rob her of the Romantic experience of adolescence. By removing Rapunzel's means of beauty,[7] the sorceress legitimates her own ugliness and demonstrates how it is synecdoche for the pure evil she embodies. This reading problematizes Rosenkranz's contention that aesthetics must assume the "concept of evil" in order to "[express] morally ugly content" because the witch is acting evilly. Rather than assuming ugliness based on morality, the tale manufactures it from the outside, from what Rosenkranz refers to as "the radical, the absolute, the ethically and religiously ugly." In the reversal emblematic in so many of

---

6   Rapunzel must be beautiful, in other words, for the tale to be tragic.

7   This is clearly a sexualized beauty, which warrants a more detailed discussion beyond the scope of this essay.

these witch narratives, the witch is ultimately the figure who loses, her ugliness paving the way for her humiliation, when she eventually finds out that Rapunzel and the Prince "lived happily and contentedly for a long time thereafter."

If we are to believe, as Plotinus maintains in the *Enneads*, that "Ugliness and evil are basically one," where do we situate the sorceress, who is neither conventionally ugly nor conventionally evil, but whose defamation as being so is manufactured from the consciousness of the tale itself? The sorceress is used as a pedagogic project that associates the corrupted femininity of staying single forever and the inability to produce offspring with the denial of traditional beauty conventions. "Rapunzel" signals, in other words, that rejecting beauty and rejecting the traditional project of the bourgeois family are critical threats to the world order. It warns children that *any* rejection of the norms of socialization (specifically those outlined by Grimm) will carry the same effects. This is a useful narrative strategy that positions the Fairy Tale within its distinctly pedagogic confines. Zipes himself would later uphold how "fairy tales operate ideologically to indoctrinate children so that they will conform to dominant social standards." The sorceress *becomes* evil in the nineteenth century reader's imagination as they engage in her witchcraft (I'm hard pressed to even refer to it as such) by reading the tale and simultaneously engaging in a profound realization that any transgression of social norms outlined in their world order will carry grave consequences—among which is ugliness. Ugliness becomes a coded punishment—a visible marker of transgression—for any of the social ills demonstrated in the tale and the conventional society they seek to represent. As Zipes points out, "To have a fairy tale published is like a symbolic announcement, an intercession on behalf of oneself, of children, of civilization. It is a historical statement." Within this logic, the two archetypes blend together to produce a moral judgement on the sorceress' soul: she is not only an unsuccessful mother, but she's also a deeply flawed, proto-evil figure who fails because her will isn't strong enough to endure the world she inhabits. Ultimately, she's destroyed by being forgotten, written out of the Grimm's history, which as Zipes maintains, is desperately "in need of a text" of its own in order to function. This physical and textual death offers a new perspective on the pedagogy of the tale.

Socialization and Sexual Anxiety in "Hansel and Gretel"

In "Hansel and Gretel," the witch is physically destroyed through an act of glorious violence that is meant to be celebrated.[8] The tale concludes that she is a victim of her own treachery, unlike the symbolic end the sorceress faces in "Rapunzel," where she is destroyed by being written out of the narrative in lieu of celebrating the young couple.

Hansel and Gretel first meet the witch as they hallucinate out of hunger and find themselves eating a "little house that was made of bread" with "cake for a roof and pure sugar for windows." She is a "very old woman leaning on a crutch" who comes "slinking out of the house." We assume that her appearance "tremendously frightened" the siblings because of her demonstrable ugliness. The witch "only pretended to be friendly" and confirms our suspicions that she had "built the house made of bread only to lure them to her," to "kill, cook, and eat them."

---

8   Though many writers have addressed the celebration of violence in the fairy tale proper, none have done it the academic justice that Scott Harshbarger has, whose critical scholarship greatly contributed to my research and exploration of this topic.

This is later complicated by one of the only salient descriptions of the association between ugliness and evil in the Brothers Grimm: "Now, witches have red eyes and cannot see very far, but they have a keen sense of smell, like animals, and can detect when human beings are near." The witch is shortsighted both physically and figuratively—she cannot see beyond her plan to "kill, cook, and eat," which will ultimately lead to her own destruction, outwitted and humiliated by two children.

"Hansel and Gretel" presents the witch as a figure deeply anxious about gathering and consuming food. In fact, the entire tale is a commentary on the socio-historical narrative of food consumption. This reading positions the witch as partially human while also demonizing her for the meal she desires: the children. As Scott Harshbarger points out, scholars have suggested different ways of classifying these concerns, including Victor Nell's point that the language used to describe losing oneself while reading is "strongly oral," linking our desire for prose with the witch's desire for food and Po-chia Hsia's historical reading of the Anti-Semitic hysteria and mythology behind food shortages in early modern Europe projected onto Jewish "ritual child murder" and the "practice of abducting Christian children for their Satanic rituals." These readings represent the hysteria surrounding the witch's relationship with consumption of any form. Though the tale clearly carries the historical background Hsia identifies, I would complicate his argument by suggesting that its central concern of food consumption also works to vilify the witch for any physical engorgement related to eating and fattening oneself at the expense of other characters.

The elements of food consumption scattered throughout the tale tempt the witch into a ritual of consumption that would place her on equal footing with the other characters. The witch, it should be noted, doesn't struggle finding food during the famine that predicates the entire tale: whereas the children are each given one piece of bread by their parents and are trapped in a famine, the witch has the means to build an entire house of temptation out of cake and pure sugar. She even serves Hansel and Gretel a "good meal of milk and pancakes with sugar and apples and nuts" which is likely the most decadent meal they have ever eaten. Harshbarger corroborates this point, observing that "In 'Hansel and Gretel' the occasion for communal devastation is famine, a periodic scourge well known to the European peasantry," through the scholarship of Robert Darnton.[9] In the tale, the witch is conveniently placed outside of these concerns. Her access to lavish treats—and by extension her immunity from historical famine—suggests a break with the world order of the tale. This break is synonymous with Voltmer's status of the witch as the "disorderly 'other', a rebel against patriarchal, social, political, and religious order," all of which are symbolized in her access to food amidst a famine. This access reveals a temptation that she must overcome in order to transcend the world of conventional beauty she is already excluded from: the witch is encouraged to dole out the treats she owns and *simultaneously abstain* from enjoying them herself at the peril of engorging herself into fattened ugliness. She lapses into these temptations by considering the children a "'tasty meal!'" and trapping Hansel in a cage to enthusiastically feed him as if he were a pig. Her repeated tests, "'Stick out your finger so I can feel how fat you are'" and her insistence that "'I don't care whether Hansel's fat or thin. He's going to be slaughtered tomorrow,'" indicate how the temptation of food consumption has finally taken hold of her. Morally, this conclusion can be read as a warning against overindulging in the temptations of

---

9   See Darnton's *The Great Cat Massacre* (2009).

German cuisine. But inside the text, it functions to vilify the witch for losing control over her most primal urges and succumbing to the desire to fatten herself at the literal expense of these children's bodies.

It is in opposition with this detail, then, that we must read her violent destruction. Gretel, who tricks the witch into walking into the oven, "gave her a push that sent her flying inside and shut the iron door and bolted it. *Whew!* The witch began to howl dreadfully, but Gretel ran away, and the godless witch was miserably burned to death." This destruction raises questions about the celebration of violence given the young audience the fairy tales assume—which social reality, if any, warrants such a celebration of murder? For Scott Harshbarger, the witch's annihilation "[is] necessary for the fulfillment of the canonical utopian script" of the genre writ large. She is in a "direct relationship with ultimate evil," and thus, must be destroyed. The children, Gretel in particular, is credited with a "superior mind-reading [ability]" and is lauded for her creativity at the expense of burning another human being. Readers are even encouraged to rationalize the evil Gretel temporarily demonstrates as a moment of pure cunning. But what she destroys (albeit without knowing) extends beyond the corporeal body of an ostracized, 'ugly' woman: by forcing the burning of the witch, the logic of the tale depicts an instance in which children outwitting adults in conventional society is acceptable so long as it rids that society of a perceived evil, an ugly elderly woman, and leaves the children in an equally transitory status appropriate for their age where "all their troubles were over." The ugly woman, who already inconveniences the world of the tale because she is immune from the famine, is justly destroyed rather than tolerated. This rhetorical move socializes children into a world in which it's acceptable to exploit the Ugly to the point of violence. It's no longer enough for the characters to humiliate the witch, as in "Rapunzel." Instead, the goal becomes to completely destroy her. This extends Rosenkranz's thesis on the evil of ugliness to its logical (nevertheless terrifying end) in which the destruction of anything—even human life—is acceptable so long as that life does not harmonize with the bourgeois, heteronormative discourse of feminine beauty in which the tales are written. At the start of the tale, the witch embodies the social evil of gluttony, a very real evil given the historical famines and food shortages of early modern Europe, and ends physically disembodied through pain, the end-by-revenge whereby she can feast no more.

The Future of Ugliness

The militarization of ugliness against these women reveals a host of male anxieties about the status of women in society. It is beyond the scope of this essay to enumerate all of them, but it should be noted that these anxieties, which may have been founded on suspicion, had very little supporting evidence given the hindsight contemporary scholarship affords. As Voltmer posits, "the vast majority of people across Europe who were accused of being witches never attempted to conduct harmful magic against their accusers." The anxiety over a witch making houses out of sugar seems demonstrably hollow. But the effects of the reactionary hysteria shouldn't be minimized.

What, then, of the future of ugliness? It might seem preposterous to propose—much less consider—the future of what seems to be a trivial question. But as I hope to have demonstrated in this essay, these questions are responsible for redirecting the course of women's lives, and, if we assume the mass audience of the Fairy Tale, the attitudes of entire impressionable generations. Little could be as damaging as inculcating a belief that the ugly and the evil are synonymous, yet these distinctions are seldom clear throughout these tales. In fact, during the early modern witch trials, these beliefs destroyed thousands of human lives.[10] Today, in a world where the privileging of beauty is finally encountering serious socio-cultural resistance through the salient questions Ugly Scholarship is posing, it's helpful to propose a few implications for the future of ugliness as it's developed in the Brothers Grimm and then recast in the twenty-first century.

1. *We have yet to escape the ugly-woman-as-witch paradigm.* The Witch label may no longer be militarized against entire groups of people, forcing them to the outside of society, but the same dynamics of social exclusion are still alive today. As Voltmer demonstrates, The Witch was created by "all-inclusive stereotyping of enemies from within and without [that] was broad enough to label even the smallest conflicts within families and households,…as evidence of witchcraft." Today, The Witch can be figured as a threatening political adversary, its label used and abused with little understanding of the very real historical consequences this label once carried.[11]

---

10   See Rita Voltmer, "The Witch Trials." *The Oxford Illustrated History of Witchcraft and Magic*, edited by Owen Davies, Oxford University Press, 2017, pp. 97-133.

11   This calls to mind President Trump's recent tweets claiming he is the victim of a "Phony Witch Hunt" (@realDonaldTrump 7 May 2018) and a "Russian Witch Hunt" (@realDonaldTrump 7 May 2018). These situations define the future of The Witch project.

2. *The reclamation of ugliness, something unimaginable in the pedagogic logic of the tales, has today become part of a proto-feminist movement.* Fatness, which has often been coded as ugliness, is today given a platform through the "Fat Pride Movement," which is predicated on "[fat people] trying to live a life with dignity." This movement attempts to disband the assumption that fatness is synonymous with ugliness by calling for dignity. Although socially productive, it has also been positioned at odds with arguments on conventional health standards.[12]

3. *Teaching children to associate evil with ugliness is inescapable in the cultural logic that drives many modes of communication including fairy tales and television.* Though it is nearly impossible to dissolve these associations, we must work to understand their histories and the social implications they carry. The question posed at the beginning of this essay, *Who thought ugliness could be so fashionable?* should be read strategically depending on the context in which it is deployed. It may be fashionable for Ugly Duck Coffee to capitalize on the slogan "Let's get ugly," but it behooves us to understand just how quickly this dynamic has been used against those who transgress the same beauty standards Ugly Duck proudly (and successfully) markets. As a recent article in Aeon demonstrates in its title alone, "The history of ugliness shows that there is no such thing." The strain of cultural relativism these questions assume is en vogue and while the article's point that "Western traditions often set ugliness in opposition to beauty, but

---

12   See Rachelle Hampton, "The Fat Pride Movement Promotes Dignity, Not a 'Lifestyle.'" *Slate*, 11 April 2018. Accessed 28 April 2018.

the concept carries positive meanings in different cultural contexts" is historically accurate, it should also be noted how the label of 'ugly' has been strategically used and abused to condemn the weak, the disfigured, and the Other.

If what I have presented as "Ugly Scholarship" is to survive and continue exerting a considerable influence on questions of witchcraft and its relationship to beauty, it must lend an increasingly analytic perspective to what once seemed like a trivial question. Although beauty can be framed as a question outside the concerns of academia, it would be a mistake to assume the same of ugliness, which has too often been presented in Burke's traditional definition. As early as 1942, L.H. Stimmel even suggested that ugliness as a literary device will hold a place in the future of American literature, "As a literary device [that] has not really established itself in the excepted masterpieces" presenting ugliness, in other words, with literary utility. Even Isidore Stern, whose writing evokes a conservative panic over the elevation of ugliness, contributes to this discourse: "[E]ven those who reside outside asylums, now find delight in the ugliness manifested by such present-day crazes as pop-art, the theater of the absurd, rock n' roll, and 4-letter words." In order to maximize its rhetorical work, the future of ugliness must be considered separate from the primary concerns of beauty—blending yet moving past the hegemony of the beautiful to seriously question how, when, and why the beautiful competed for control—and managed to displace the Ugly.

Works Cited and Consulted

Performing the Roma Witch: Stereotype, Mythology, and Profit

"A Tax on Witches? A Pox on the President." *The Associated Press*, 6 January 2011, www.nyti.ms/2KF0mbM.

Abramson, Jill. *Merchants of Truth: The Business of News and the Fight for Facts*. Simon & Schuster, 2019.

"About." *Milène Larsson*, milenelarsson.com/pages/about.

Achim, Viorel. *The Roma in Romanian History*. Budapest: Central European Press, 2004.

"Antigypsyium – A Reference Paper." *Alliance Against Antigypsyism*, 1 June 2017, www.antigypsyism.eu/wp-content/uploads/2017/07/Antigypsyism-reference-paper-16.06.2017.pdf.

"Authorize." OED Online, Oxford University Press, December 2018, www.oed.com/viewdictionaryentry/Entry/11125. Accessed 1 January 2019.

Barry, *Cultures of Witchcraft in Europe from the Middle Ages to the Present*. Springer International Publishing, 2017.

"Being a 'Gypsy': The Worst Social Stigma in Romania." *European Roma Rights Centre*, n.d. www.errc.org/roma-rights-journal/being-a-gypsy-the-worst-social-stigma-in-romania.

Beissinger, Margaret. "Occupation and Ethnicity: Constructing Identity among Professional Romani (Gypsy) Musicians in Romania." *Slavic Review*, vol. 60, no. 1, 2001, pp. 24-49.

Berger, Helen and Douglas Ezzy. "Mass Media and Religious Identity:

A Case Study of Young Witches." *Journal for the Scientific Study of Religion*, vol. 48, no. 3, 2009, pp. 501-514.

Bernstein, Lisa. "Demythifying the Witch's Identity as Social Critique in Maryse Condé's *I, Tituba, Black Witch of Salem*." *Social Identities*, vol. 3, no. 1, 1997, pp. 77-89.

Bever, Edward. "Witchcraft Prosecutions and the Decline of Magic." *Journal of Interdisciplinary History*, vol. 40, no. 2, 2009, pp. 263-293.

Bødker, Henrik. "Vice Medic Inc.: Youth Lifestyle – and News." *Journalism*, vol. 18. no. 1, 2017, pp. 27-43.

Boia, Lucian. *History and Myth in Romanian Consciousness*. Central European University Press, 2001.

Brooks, Ethel. "Europe is Ours: A Manifesto." *European Roma Rights Centre*, n.d. www.errc.org/news/europe-is-ours-a-manifesto.

Budai, Ion. *The Gypsiad. Asymptote*, www.asymptotejournal.com/poetry/ion-budai-deleanu-the-gypsiad/.

"Casting Curses and Love Spells with the Most Powerful Witches in Romania." *YouTube*, uploaded by Broadly, 31 October 2016, www.youtube.com/watch?v=X1g3CYbsssw&t=101s.

Coleman, Sandfort and Aleksandar Štulhofer. *Sexuality and Gender in Postcommunist Eastern Europe and Russia*. Haworth Press, 2005.

Corduneanu, Ioana and Nicolae-Sorin Dragan. "Semiotics of White Space on the Romanian Traditional Blouse, the IA." *Romanian Journal of Communication and Public Relations*, vol. 18, no. 3, 2016, pp. 49-63.

"Corruption Perceptions Index 2014: Results." *Transparency International*, 2014, www.transparency.org/cpi2014/results.

Cotofană, Alexandra. "Documentary Film and Magic in Communist Romania." *Open Theology*, vol. 3. no. 1, 2017, pp. 198-210.

Cotofană, Alexandra. *Governing with Magic: Politics and Labors of the Occult in Romania*. 2018. Indiana University, PhD Dissertation.

Cotofană, Alexandra. "Reinventing Witchcraft: Romanian Politics and the Occult" *LeftEast*, 30 May 2018, www.criticatac.ro/lefteast/reinventing-witchcraft-romanian-politics-and-the-occult/. Accessed 1 January 2019.

Cotofană, Alexandra. "White Man Law versus Black Magic Women. Racial and Gender Entanglements of Witchcraft Policies in Romania." *KULTU RA IR VISUOMENE . Socialiniu tyrimu žurnalas*, vol. 8, no. 2, 2017, pp. 69-95.

Čvorović, Jelena. "Serbian Gypsy Witch Narratives: 'Wherever Gypsies Go, There the Witches Are, We Know!'" *Folklore*, vol. 124, no. 2, 2013, pp. 214-225.

Federici, Silvia. *Caliban and the Witch: Women, the Body and Primitive Accumulation*. Brooklyn: Autonomedia, 2004.

Federici, Silvia. *Witches, Witch-Hunting, and Women*. PM Press, 2018.

Fehér, Andrea. "Women, Crime and the Secular Court in Eighteenth Century Cluj." *Journal of Education Culture and Society*, no. 2, 2015, 33-42.

French, Lorely. "'If we didn't have this story, we would not have this day': Roma 'Gypsy' Stories as Sustenance in Difficult Life Stages." *Pacific Coast Philology*, vol. 49, no. 1, 2014, pp. 5-24.

Gaskill, Malcolm. *Witchcraft: A Very Short Introduction*. Oup Oxford, 2010.

Hesz, Ágnes. "The Making of a Bewitchment Narrative." *Folklore*, vol. 37, 2007, 18-34.

Humphrey, Caroline. "Shamanic Practices and the State in Northern Asia: views from the Centre and Periphery." In *Shamanism, History and the State*, edited by Nicholas Thomas and Caroline Humphrey, University of Michigan Press, 1994, 191-228.

Kakissis, Joanna. "In The Land Of Dracula, Witches Work As 'Life Coaches' Of The Supernatural." *NPR*, 24 October 2018, www.npr. org/2018/10/24/660294590/in-the-land-of-dracula-witches-work-as-life-coaches-of-the-supernatural. Accessed 1 January 2019.

Kaneva, Nadia and Delia Popescu. "'We are Romanian, not Roma': Nation Branding and Postsocialist Discourses of Alterity." *Communication, Culture, & Critique*, vol. 7, no. 1, 2013, pp. 506-523.

Karasz, Palko. "In Romania, Corruption's Tentacles Grip Daily Life." *New York Times*, 9 February 2017, www.nyti.ms/2kRrDhd. Accessed 1 May 2018.

Keating, Joshua. "Romanian Witches Cast Dark Spells on Government in Tax Protest." *Foreign Policy Magazine*, 5 January 2011, www. foreignpolicy.com/2011/01/05/romanian-witches-cast-dark-spells-on-government-in-tax-protest/. Accessed 1 May 2018.

Kelly, Kim. "Are Witches the Ultimate Feminists?" *The Guardian*, 5 July 2017, www.theguardian.com/books/2017/jul/05/witches-feminism-books-kristin-j-sollee.

Klainiczay, Gábor and Éva Pócs. *Witchcraft and Demonology in Hungry and Transylvania*. Springer, 2017.

Kraidy, Marwan. *Hybridity, Or the Cultural Logic of Globalization*. Temple University Press, 2005.

Leland, Charles Godfrey. *Gypsy Sorcery and Fortune Telling*. Forgotten Books, 2008.

"Mădălin-Ştefan Voicu Curriculum Vitae." *Camera Deputatilor*, n.d. www.cdep.ro/pls/parlam/structura. mp?idm=322&cam=2&leg=2000&pag=0&idl=1.

Mar, Alex. *Witches of America*. Farrar, Straus, and Giroux, 2016.

March, Andrew. "Is Vice's Documentary on ISIS Illegal?" *The Atlantic*, 1 October 2014, www.theatlantic.com/international/archive/2014/10/is-vice-documentary-on-ISIS-illegal/380991/. Accessed 1 January 2019.

McGarry, Aidan. "Roma as a Political Identity: Exploring Representations of Roma in Europe." *Sage Publications*, vol. 14. no. 6, 2014, pp. 756-774.

Mendizabel, Isabel. "Reconstructing the Population History of European Romani from Genome-wide Data." *Current Biology*, vol. 22, no. 24, 2012, pp. 2342-2349.

Merchant, Carolyn. *The Death of Nature: Women, Ecology, and the Scientific Revolution*. HarperOne, 1990.

Miller, William. "Class Lecture." English 440: The Witch, 2 April 2018. Lecture.

Mitchell, Joseph Miller. "King of Gypsies." *The New Yorker*, 15 August 1942, www.archives.newyorker.com/?i=1942-08-15#folio=CV1. Accessed 1 January 2019.

Mutler, Alison. "Romania's Witches Curse Income Tax Ruling." *The Associated Press*, 5 January 2011, www.nbcnews.com/id/40930813/ns/business-world_business/t/romanias-witches-curse-income-tax-ruling/#.WvxlnS-ZMWo. Accessed 1 May 2018.

"National Roma Integration Strategies: A First Step In the Implementation of the EU Framework." *European Commission*, 21 May 2012, www.ec.europa.eu/anti-trafficking/sites/antitrafficking/files/national_roma_integration_strategies_a_first_step_in_the_implementation_of_the_eu_framework.pdf

"O Scurta Istorie A Tiganilor (TOTUL DESPRE TOT)." *YouTube*, uploaded by Totul Despre Tot Oficial, 6 September 2016, www.youtube.com/watch?v=P1IxsomP1qE&t=553s&frags=pl%2Cwn.

"On The Line: Milène Larsson Discusses Europe's Migrant Crisis" *YouTube*, uploaded by VICE News, 26 October 2015, https://www.youtube.com/watch?v=W0lhcjC8Lzg

Penny, Laurie. "Witch Kids of Instagram." *The Baffler*, 13 December 2017, www.thebaffler.com/war-of-nerves/witch-kids-of-instagram.

Pop-Curseu, Ioan. "The Gypsy-Witch: Social-Cultural Representations, Fascination and Fears." *Journal of Ethnography and Folklore*, vol. 1, no. 2, 2014, pp. 23-45.

Pop, Cornelia and Nicolae Marinescu. *Romania as a Tourist Destination and the Romanian Hotel Industry*. Cambridge Scholars Publishing, 2007.

"Poverty and Employment: The Situation of Roma in 11 EU Member States." *European Union Agency for Fundamental Rights*, 1 October 2014, www.fra.europa.eu/en/publication/2014/poverty-and-employment-situation-roma-11-eu-member-states.

"Roma Health Mediators: Successes and Challenges." *Roma Health Project: Open Society Public Health Program*, 1 October 2011, www.opensocietyfoundations.org/sites/default/files/roma-health-mediators-20111022.pdf.

"Romania's Roma: The Art of Exclusion." *The Economist*, 20 February 2015, www.economist.com/news/2015/02/20/the-art-of-exclusion.

"Romania's Roma: Where is Europe's Roma Policy?" *The Economist*, 19 September 2012, www.economist.com/eastern-approaches/2012/09/19/where-is-europes-roma-policy.

Roper, Lyndal. *The Witch in the Western Imagination*. University of Virginia Press, 2012.

Roper, Trevor H.R. *The European Witch Craze of the Sixteenth and Seventeenth Centuries*. HarperCollins College Division, 1969.

Simpson, Connor. "Why Is Vice Hiding Its Kim Jong-Un Interview?" *The Atlantic*, 17 June 2013, www.theatlantic.com/international/archive/2013/06/why-vice-hiding-its-kim-jong-un-interview/314174/. Accessed 1 January 2019.

Sollée, Kristen. *Witches, Sluts, Feminists: Conjuring the Sex Positive*. 2017, Stone Bridge Press.

Stan, Lavinia. "Witch-hunt or Moral Rebirth?: Romanian Parliamentary Debates on Lustation." *East European Politics and Societies*, vol. 26, no. 2, 2012, pp. 274-295.

Szeman, *Staging Citizenship: Roma, Performance and Belonging in EU Romania*. Berghahn Books, 2017.

"The Grammar of Hard Facts." *The Economist*, 14 May 2015, www. economist.com/books-and-arts/2015/05/14/the-grammar-of-hard-facts

"The Witch Continues to Enchant as a Feminist Symbol." *New York Times*, 31 October 2018, www.nytimes.com/2018/10/31/t-magazine/witch-feminist-symbol.html

United States, Court of Appeals for the Fourth Circuit. *Herbert Daniel Dettmer v. Robert Landon*. Docket no. 799-729, 4 September 1986. *United States Court of Appeals for the Fourth Circuit*, www.law.justia.com/cases/federal/appellate-courts/F2/799/929/117777/

Vice News. "How to Contact Us." www.news.Vice.com/en_us/page/how-to-contact-us

Vice News. www.news.vice.com/en_us

Walker, Sarah-Houghton. *Representations of the Gypsy in the Romantic Period*. Oxford University Press, 2014.

Wiedeman, Reeves. "A Company Built on a Bluff." *New York Magazine*. 10 June 2018, www.nymag.com/intelligencer/2018/06/inside-vice-media-shane-smith.html. Accessed 1 January 2019.

The Fairy Tale and the Aesthetics of Ugliness

Aristotle. "Poetics." *Classical Literary Criticism*, edited by Penelope Murray and T. S. Dorsch, Penguin Group, 2000, pp. 57-97.

Burke, Edmund. *On the Sublime and Beautiful*. New York, Harvard Classics, 2001.

Darnton, Robert. *The Great Cat Massacre*. New York, Basic Books, 2009.

Hampton, Rachelle. "The Fat Pride Movement Promotes Dignity, Not a 'Lifestyle.'" *Slate*, 11 April 2018. Accessed 28 April 2018.

Harshbarger, Scott. "Grimm and Grimmer: 'Hansel and Gretel' and Fairy Tale Nationalism." *Style*, vol. 47, no. 4, 2013, pp. 490-508.

Henderson, Gretchen. "The history of ugliness shows that there is no such thing." *Aeon*, 8 March 2016. Accessed 28 April 2018.

"Malleus Maleficarum." *Sacred Texts*, 2011, www.sacred-texts.com/pag/

mm/

Nell, Victor. *Lost in a Book: The Psychology of Reading for Pleasure*. New Haven, Yale UP, 1988.

Plotinus. "Enneads." *The Bloomsbury Anthology of Aesthetics*, edited by Joseph Tanke and Colin McQuillan, Bloomsbury Academic, 2017, pp. 55-61.

Rosenkranz, Karl. *Aesthetic of Ugliness*. New York, Bloomsbury Academic, 2015.

Sharpe, James. "The Demonologists." *The Oxford Illustrated History of Witchcraft* and Magic, edited by Owen Davies, Oxford University Press, 2017, pp. 65-96.

Stemmler, Joan. "The Physiognomical Portraits of Johann Caspar Lavater." *The Art Bulletin*, vol. 75, no. 1, 1993, pp. 151-168.

Stern, Isidore. "The Cult of Ugliness." *The North American Review*, vol. 250, no. 5/6, 1965, pp. 28-30.

Stimmel, L. H. "Our Ugly Contemporaries." *College English*, vol. 3, no. 5, 1942, pp. 454-459.

Voltmer, Rita. "The Witch Trials." *The Oxford Illustrated History of Witchcraft* and Magic, edited by Owen Davies, Oxford University Press, 2017, pp. 97-133.

Zipes, Jack. "Hansel and Gretel." *The Complete Fairy Tales of the Brothers Grimm*, edited by Jack Zipes, Bantam Books, 2003, pp. 53-58.

Zipes, Jack. "Rapunzel." *The Complete Fairy Tales of the Brothers Grimm*, edited by Jack Zipes, Bantam Books, 2003, pp. 42-45.

Zipes, Jack. *Fairy Tales and the Art of Subversion*. New York, Routledge, 2012.

Appendix

Fig. 1 (0:30) Opening credits of *Vice News*' 2016 film "Casting Curses and Love Spells with the Most Powerful Witches in Romania." From these credits alone, it's clear that *Vice* is playing to an established witchcraft tradition meant to help socialize the audience into the text they present.

Fig. 2 (0:09) The opening credits fade to an image of the witches who will form the subject of the film. Pictured here is the witches' sabbath, a common trope related to witch iconography complete with the burning witch's broom and the cauldron fire. Notice that all figures pictured above are women, wearing white, and a majority are holding a candle.

Fig. 3 (0:10) The broom is dipped into the cauldron fire, lit, and then moved through the air with a clear goal being to create a spectacle out of the moment. While this happens, the witches recite the first of many curses they will continue to develop throughout the film.

Fig. 4 (1:19) The interviewer, Milène Larsson, pictured upon her arrival at the Minca family's home in Mogoșoaia, just outside the capital city, Bucharest. In many ways, Larsson is the typical candidate for a *Vice* interviewer, imparting her clearly Westernized fashion, language, and style of speech to the film. I will have more to say about this when I present a critique of *Vice News* founded on the form of Westernized cosmopolitanism it imparts.

Fig. 5 and 6 (1:45) Assorted witch paraphernalia presented at the beginning of the film. This is done to frame the audience's interpretations of the witchcraft they are about to experience within a well-established tradition of tarot and voodoo. There is little that leads me to believe that either of these artifacts is distinctly Romanian.

Fig. 7 and 8 (2:11, 2:36) Mihaela Minca, the main witch to be interviewed in the film, who takes Larsson and the camera crew around her property, answers their questions, and allows them to experience what it means to "cast curses and love spells" with the witches of Mogoșoaia. Throughout the film, Minca is very careful to control her image, both through the deliberate actions she takes to dress like a witch (see the garments she wears above as well as the one laying on the couch in Fig. 7) she aims to be and through the language she uses to express herself.

Fig. 9 (2:46) Larsson is later transformed into a witch, dressed more appropriately now to "cast curses and love spells" with the other witches. I will have more to say about this fashion transformation later. In the background is the Minca family property.

Fig. 10 (3:50) Left to right: Minca, her daughter, and Larsson gathered by the cauldron as they prepare their first herbal spell. Larsson is cautious to partake in the ritual, positioning herself to the left of the cauldron and watching rather than partaking directly in the action. Again, traditional witch iconography is present—the cauldron is prepared and herbs are gathered in baskets.

Fig. 11 and 12 (5:15, 5:23) Minca being recognized at the Congress of Witches organized by Ion Iliescu in 1976. It has been difficult to trace the historical accuracy of this congress' proceedings. Nevertheless, it represents a clear blurring between the licit and illicit magic sanctioned by the Romanian government.

Fig. 13 (6:11) Bratara Buzea, known as "one of the most powerful witches in the world" according to speculation in the film, sharing the anecdote of when she was jailed for practicing witchcraft during Ceaușescu's regime. Buzea shares, "Under Ceaușescu we weren't allowed to practice witchcraft. We would do everything secretly. I was tracked down and sent to prison. I wasn't scared. I beat him up, the police man. I took the bat and beat him up. He wanted to take my money, my tarot cards, but he couldn't. I served six months in prison and then came home." It is well-documented that Ceaușescu was paranoid about witchcraft, though is rumored to have kept and consulted a personal witch, *Mama Omida* or Mother Caterpillar. This and other speculations have remained difficult to verify.

Fig. 14 (10:38) A woman who visits Minca for a consultation and cites unpleasant nightmares she has been experiencing. Minca performs a spell with the chicken and then scarifies it before the audience, telling the woman here for the consultation, "The bird is dead. It died instead of you."

Fig. 15 (12:39) An advertisement posted outside Minca's home describing her as "Romania's most powerful witch." This advertisement begs the question—just how many other witches are there?

believing something might happen to them.

Fig. 16 (15:27) Alin Popoviciu in his office while being interviewed by Larsson about the tax on witches. Popoviciu claims
that the tax was never passed because some of his colleagues
were worried the witches would retaliate and hex them: "Some
of my colleagues had encounters with witches. They preferred
not to pass this law, believing something might happen to them."
This comment represents one of the most obvious blends of licit
and illicit magic sanctioned by the Romanian government and
serves as the foundation for my argument that taxes sanction
Roma witchcraft by partially proving its validity in the eyes
of the law.

Acknowledgments

Although the energy required to sustain a full-time graduate education while also working full-time necessitated an inordinate amount of dedication and caffiene, it would be a mistake not to thank the dozens of people who—passing in and out of my consciousness across this past year—gave their time and money, sent their thoughts in my direction, or just stopped by to share a laugh. First and foremost, I thank my parents, Greta and Octavian, who financially supported my education. Thank you for seeing me down the path I had always wanted to take and lighting the way—brightly. I hope you can see that the value I've found in this work would be impossible without the value you saw in supporting my education.

My brother, Octavian, his wife, Joshana. Again, for financially making my education possible while also supplying the necessary laughs and conversations required to sustain my sanity. Thank you for being the greatest of friends and the greatest of guides. And for Neo, who previewed preliminary arguments made in this book while on summer vacation in between breaks spent searching for the Witch of Ellicot Creek.

My grandma, Valentina, who taught high school courses in Russian and Romanian and who still writes, to this day, well into her ninetieth year. Without her, there would have been no Da Gheorghita. I am continually reminded about the way family resemblances skip generations. In you, I found my own literary teaching career.

My first college professor and mentor, Wesp. I cannot forget the day we installed an espresso machine in your office so that we could hold our weekly chats in comfort. This book is dedicated to you in acknowledgement for the immeasurable effect you've had on my career.

My advisor, Dr. William Miller, whose class I credit with sparking the witch interest. Thank you for guiding my research and writing, and helping me produce solid academic work. And Dr. Sarah Higley, who graciously served as a second reader for this project.

Corinne, for your kindness and love, and for always finding and sharing a new part of witch culture for us to talk about. Thank you for being so perceptive and encouraging.

Lauren, Mallory, Madeline, Kelly, Jillian, and Danielle, friends who encouraged my interests in witches while also making light of the fact that—witches, really?

Finally, my students, driven individuals who continue to dazzle me with their interpretations of the literature we read and authors we study.

About the Author

George Goga teaches literature and writing in upstate New York and owns Dapper Sloth Editing and Proofreading, which specializes in preparing novels, non-fiction, and academic manuscripts for publication. His company has worked with clients across the legal, academic, and medical fields. He is the author of *Essays at the Intersection of Literature and Pop Culture* and the forthcoming *With No Segue Whatsoever* and writes regularly for *The Public Buffalo*.

Made in the USA
Middletown, DE
26 May 2019